𝔚est 𝕮ork - *"a sort of a history, like..."*

Tony Brehony

KB
KESTREL BOOKS

Published by

Kestrel Books Ltd.

48a Main st., Bray, Co. Wicklow, Ireland.
Tel: 01 2863402, Fax: 01 286 0984

Printed by Falcon Print & Finish Ltd.
Bray, Co. Wicklow, Ireland.

First Published 1997

ISBN 1 900505 15 0

Dedicated to the memory
of my late wife, Phyl.
Our last holiday together was spent in West Cork.

DRAWN BY H. NELSON

R. CLAYTON. Sc

iv

"The history of a town, or a locality,
is often but the history of a nation in miniature."

- G. Bennett

Preface

hat is sometimes presented as history quite often is nothing more than fable and myth passed down through the centuries and inevitably filtered or polluted by local and biased interpretation.

To shoulder the task of presenting the history of such a diverse region of Ireland as West Cork makes the writer's task even more formidable.

Here for centuries English settlers battled it out with the so-called brigands and raparees they dismissed derisively as the *"meer Irishry."*

The Irish for their part were lorded over by Clan Chieftains many of whom treated them no better then the hated English settlers.

And when the English *"became more Irish than the Irish themselves"* and religion became part of the equation, then suddenly it was Protestants fighting Papists and the waters get so muddied that the researcher's task becomes well nigh impossible. What is truth and what is fiction? It matters not - the tales told by both sides are still presented as history.

I suggest that you look on this work not as a history but as a series of searching essays about the West Cork we all love. Keep an open mind and don't allow national or native sentiment to fog the vision as we look back down the centuries.

History is a two faced jade; trust her not.

List of Illustrations

Table of Contents

1

The Dawn

t was the year of Our Lord, 1588 and Elizabeth, the Virgin Queen sat on the throne of England. The bloody Geraldine rebellion was over and its leaders were hounded and hunted throughout the length and breadth of Munster and beyond. Soon, the head of the Earl of Desmond - The Red Earl - was spiked, a ghastly trophy, on London Bridge. His brother, Sir James, was tried by court-martial, his body drawn and quartered and his head set up over one of the gates of Cork. Another brother, Sir John, had his head cut off and put on display in Dublin. His mutilated body was dragged to Cork and strung up by the heels on the gibbet at North-gate. Munster, after the years of devastation and bloodshed, was a wasteland with most of its people dead or dying from starvation.

"All nearly were brought to such wretchedness," wrote Spencer, *"as that any stoney heart must rue the same. Out of every corner of the woods and glynnes they came creeping forth upon their handes, for their legges could not bear them. They looked like anatomies of death; they spoke like ghosts, crying out of their grave; they did eat the dead carrion, happy when they could find them."*

Counting the cost of the years of rebellion in Ireland, Elizabeth declared that she *"would encourage and enable our loving subjects of good behaviour, and account, within our realms of England, to inhabit and re-people a great part of the province of Munster which through the late rebellion of the Earl of Desmond and others his confederates, as by forfeiture and other lawful means, sundry lordships, manors, lands, tenements, and hereditaments within the province, have come into our hands..."*

All this land which she declared forfeit to the crown amounted to 547,628 acres and her ambitious plan was that, within a year or two, it would be inhabited by twenty thousand families. The settlers, she decreed, were to be English and Protestant, and their heirs were to marry none but of English birth. These settlers were not to permit any of *"the meer Irishry"* to be maintained in any of their families.

Chieftain Conor O'Mahony of Castle-Mahon in the County of Cork was of royal blood, a descendent of Olioll Olum, a King of Munster who died in 234 AD. When the Lord Lieutenant, Sir Henry Sidney, visited Cork in 1575 he described O'Mahony dismissively as *"a man of small force"*. However, this small force, twenty-six horse and one hundred and twenty men, played a leading role in the Geraldine rebellion when O'Mahony enthusiastically backed the Earl of Desmond in his bloody attempt to cast off the English yoke. Unfortunately, at the early age of 23 he was killed in battle. And now, even in death, he was to pay a further price - the forfeiture of his castle at Castle-Mahon, and his lands which lay for several miles on both sides of the river Bandon. The castle and 14,000 acres of land were conferred on Phane Beecher, son of Alderman Henry Beecher of London.

The Patent. which is dated September 30th, 1588, grants to *"Phane Beecher of London the Castle of O'Mahony and the moiety of all the lands and hereditaments therein - 14,000 acres - at a yearly rent of £66 13s 4d."* By the conditions of the patent, Beecher was bound to *"erect, or cause to be erected, houses for four score and eleven - ninety one families in all."*

Soon, shipload after shipload of settlers, many with their wives and children, arrived in Kinsale harbour. From there they made their weary way on foot along a bridle path through deeply wooded country along the northern banks of the river Bandon till they reached a ford. There they settled. The plantation of West Cork had begun.....

2

2

BANDON

About one mile east of O'Mahony's Castle-Mahon was a strip of flat land called Inis-fraoc. The Bandon river flowed in front of it and another river, the Bridewell, flowed at its rear before eventually joining the Bandon. A stream formed its western boundary. It was on this piece of land, more than 25 acres in area, that Beecher decided to build his new town. It was an ideal site. The waters which surrounded it would turn mill-wheels and, at the same time act as defensive barriers against the treacherous Irishry who might attack at any time. And the new town's proximity to Kinsale would give the settlers facilities for exporting their produce and importing the many goods and chattels required by a growing population.

The houses were constructed for quick and immediate occupation. A quarried stone gable held the fire-place and flue but the rest of the house was made of boards and plaster with a thatched roof. Soon streets ranged out in a carefully planned pattern. One of the principal streets faced the Bridewell river and another faced the Bandon. Midway, between them, was the Main Street. A further settlement was started on the opposite bank of the Bandon and a six-arch stone bridge was constructed to link the growing settlements. Beecher proudly called his new town Bandon-bridge.

One who was alive at the time that the first colonists arrived described the site of the new colony as *"a mere waste bog and wood, serving for a retreat and harbour to rebels and thieves and wolves."*

Yet, just 40 years later, the same writer tells us that Bandon-bridge was now worthy of regard *"for its bigness and its handsomeness and ranked with Kilkenny, the seat of the Confederate Government Its population, wherein are at least seven thousand souls are all of them stoutly Protestant, and the streets and houses are clean and neat and present none of that carelessness and disregard for cleanliness too often a very sad characteristic of our Irish towns and villages"*

In 1610, Lord Cork, who had been Elizabeth's Lord High Chancellor, under pressure from the inhabitants agreed that the town should be walled because of the sporadic attacks and incursions by the dispossessed Irishry who now inhabited the surrounding forest. The going rate for stonemasons at the time stood at two and a half pence per day but a militant leader of the workforce, seeing a long and possibly lucrative contract looming ahead for the masons of Cork, decided the time was ripe to demand the substantial increase of one half penny per day.

"The members of the Stonemasons' Guild will not be exploited further," he told a very irate Lord Cork, *"and no walls will guard the town of Bandon unless the just demands of the masons are conceded."* The Earl refused to be blackmailed by such idle varlets and he told them so in no uncertain terms. They could, he went on, *"betake themselves to the devil out of Bandon, and, by gad, he'd be damned in hell before he'd bow to their impudent demands."*

Lord Cork withdrew to his stately home and the masons marched off the site.

The walls of Bandon were to be built mainly of heavy black slate, about nine feet thick, varying in height from 30 to 50 feet. The area of the town enclosed was estimated at 26 English acres. There were three castles to be erected also, each containing 26 rooms, the turrets and flanks to be platformed with lead and mounted with cannon.

4

This then was the ambitious building programme undertaken by Lord Cork, but now the site was idle and deserted as the masons and the Earl played the ritual waiting game.

One mason with a sick wife and a large family to support decided that he could not afford to join his companions on strike. Lord Cork, hoping that the man's example would influence the others, agreed to let him work on alone.

Days passed into weeks. Whatever about the pressures of hunger and misery on the idle masons, the political pressures brought to bear on Lord Cork to complete the defences of Bandon became unbearable. Suddenly he pocketed his pride and capitulated, agreeing to all the demands of the striking workers. They marched back triumphantly to the site and started work at their new rate - three pennies a day.

As for the unfortunate black-leg mason, his fellow craftsmen insisted that he be instantly dismissed. Lord Cork, to his credit, refused their demand even under threat of further strike. That evening, however, the masons gathered menacingly around their erstwhile workmate and one of them, chosen by lot, hit him from behind with a pickaxe, splitting his skull and killing him instantly. They buried his body in the foundations of the walls and laid a course of masonry over it to conceal their crime for ever from the eyes of man. They nearly succeeded.

It was fully two hundred years later that workers, removing a part of the old town walls to build a summer-house for a local resident, came across a large flagstone. A quick tap of the pickaxe gave off a hollow sound. Visions of Spanish doubloons and buried treasures rose temptingly before their eyes but further investigation uncovered only the mouldering bones of the murdered mason. The fatal pickaxe lay under his smashed skull and his own hammer and trowel still lay as they had been placed the day the strike at Bandon walls had finished. By his side where his pocket might have been was a small silver coin of the reign of Edward VI, (1547 - 1553), no doubt part of the hard earned money which had cost him his life. And soon that

5

coin was all that remained - the skeleton, upon being exposed to the air, crumpled into dust.

The walls themselves too crumbled before the ravages of time. Lord Cork had boasted that the walls of Bandon were stronger, thicker, and higher then the walls of Derry and would last for ever. Today, only small lengths have survived the unrest and troubles of the intervening centuries. These sections now constitute the north wall of Kilbrogan churchyard, the south wall of Ballymodan churchyard and the wall behind the new Garda Divisional Headquarters in Weir Street.

In the winter of 1649, Cromwell delighted the loyal citizens of Bandon with a surprise visit from his headquarters in Youghal. Writes a historian of the time:

"After reviewing the garrison, he referred to the gallant Bandon Militia as the 'Fire Eaters,' by which name they were known long after the Cromwellian wars were over and peace and prosperity had returned and overspread our country with happiness and abundance."

Whatever about the loyal towns of Cork and Youghal and Bandon, the rest of Cork County, rebel as ever, paid a dear and terrible price for its opposition to the forces of Cromwell. Banishment to Hell or to Connaught, and the forfeiture of all lands was the order of the day. And the forfeiture in Cork County amounted to 98,000 acres, exceeding those of every other county except Cavan.

"The devotion of the ancient and loyal borough of Bandon to the English interest was more conspicuous than that of any other town in the whole kingdom", praised the historian, *"and there was not a seizure of a single foot of our ground."*

Because great numbers of the male population of Cork County had been slaughtered or were forced into exile to join foreign armies after the battle of Kinsale, the rebellion of 1641 and the subsequent Cromwellian campaign the numbers of women remaining behind were vastly in excess of the men. Lord Broghill, son of Lord Cork and a Christian gentleman, decided that he must, whatever the cost, save these unfortunate ladies from possible immorality, and ordered *"that Irish women, as being too numerous now, and therefore exposed to prostitution, be sold to merchants and transported to Virginia, New England, Jamaica or other countries, where they may support themselves by their labours."*

"It is not a difficult matter at this time," he informed Cromwell, *"to procure plenty of females as there are crowds of young widows and deserted wives wandering about in the vicinity of Bandon without any visible means of support."* Boys and girls were also on request, but the women were preferred, provided, he suggested, *"that they were marriageable and not past breeding."*

To carry his plans to fruition, Lord Broghill sent over agents to England and contracted with Messers Sellick & Leader of Bristol, to furnish them with two hundred and fifty women of the Irish nation, between the ages of twelve and forty-five, and three hundred men, between twelve years old and fifty. They were to be shipped at Kinsale and to be procured within twenty miles of Bandon. Lord Broghill felt sure that this would not present any great problem and he issued orders for the area to be searched for the requisite numbers of wanderers and persons who had no ostensible means of livelihood.

And so the flower of West Cork, men, women and children, were transported across the seas to sweat out their lives in the heat and misery of the sugar-cane plantations of the West Indies. The infamous curse of Cromwell had reached into their very souls.

Cromwell, in reply to a letter from Mr. Secretary Thurloe asking if he could supply a further two thousand boys from 12 to 14 years of age for use in the West Indies, had this to say:

"We could indeed well spare them, and who knows, it might even be a glorious means to make them Protestant..."

Staunch Protestantism was ever the beacon light for the proud inhabitants of Bandon. The first ever edifice built in Ireland for Protestant worship was Christ Church, Kilbrogan erected in 1610 on the site of a Danish fort known at the time as Badger's Hill. Prior to that, all the churches used for Protestant worship had been confiscated from the Catholics. Today, Christ Church still stands proudly looking down on the town of Bandon but it is now a Tourist Centre and museum housing many of the artefacts and relics of hundreds of years of Bandon history.

The story is told that a notice was permanently displayed on the gates of Bandon which proclaimed that:

"A Turk, a Jew, or an Atheist

May live in this town, but no Papist."

It is then claimed that an Irish scholar, in the dead of night, further appended the lines:

"He that wrote these lines did write them well,

As the same is written on the gates of Hell."

Fortunately or unfortunately, depending of which biased view of so-called history one takes, doubt has been cast on whether such a bigoted notice was ever displayed on the gates of Bandon. Tradition suggests that the venerable Dean Swift, on one of his frequent visits to Bandon, composed a stanza which, in fact, gave rise to the tale. The stanza, written with an uncharacteristically vituperative pen, read as follows:

"A Turk, a Jew, or an Atheist

May live in this town, but no Papist.

He that wrote these lines did write them well,

As the same is written on the gates of Hell.

For Friar Hayes, who made his exit of late,
Of pox, some say. But no matter for that -
He died; and if what we heard is aright,
He came to Hell's gates in a mournful plight.
'Who's there?' said the sentry on guard. Quote the other,
'A wretched poor priest, sir! A Catholic brother!'
'Halt! instantly halt! Avaunt! and stand clear.
Go, be damned somewhere else; you shan't be damned here!
We admit no such fellow, for a wretch so uncivil,
Who on earth would eat God, would in Hell eat the Devil!"

All wheels eventually turn full circle and in the year of Our Lord, 1796, the wheel of history turned full circle in Bandon. The foundation-stone of a Roman Catholic chapel was laid on Gallon's Hill on the 28th of April. The ground was given by the Earl of Bandon, who, in addition, subscribed liberally towards the erection of the chapel, as did many of the inhabitants of Bandon.

Just a few years later in 1807, one Paddy Gaffney, described as *"a resolute sort of fellow, albeit a Papist,"* was the first Catholic given permission to open a shop in the Main Street of Bandon in which he sold pies and mutton-broth. His Protestant neighbours, once their initial curiosity at seeing a "real live Papist" living in their midst had worn off, bore him no animosity nor ill-will and his business thrived.

Soon, other intrepid Catholics followed Paddy Gaffney's lead and merged with the Protestant population as friends and neighbours in the prosperous town of Bandon. A religious census taken in 1834 showed that the proportion of Catholics to Protestants within the walled area was almost identical. A new era, the Era of Industrialisation, had dawned and brought an upsurge of industries to the town in brewing, distilling, tanning, joinery, cotton milling, hosiery, printing and baking. To take full advantage of the opportunities now on offer and to protect their mutual economic interests, Catholics and Protestants came together to reap the potential glorious harvest with no sectarian bitterness keeping them apart.

One of the most successful industrial enterprises of the era was the Bandon Distillery, founded by Messrs. Alman.

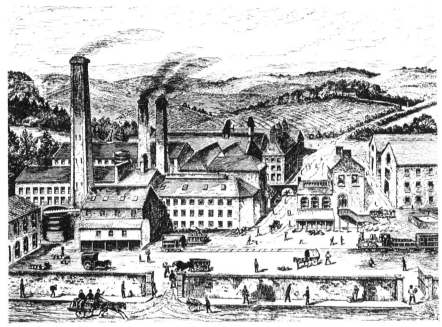

The Bandon Distillery.

"It was in ancient times", wrote Alfred Barnard in his Whiskey Distilleries of the United Kingdom, (1826), *"one of the old manorial mills and dates back to the year 1700. The main block of buildings extends some 464 feet eastwards, whilst northwards they run back 340 feet, and nearly all of them are five and six storeys .When we visited the Distillery there were up to seventy carts laden with barley, each waiting their turn to deliver, and we were informed that 1,200 barrels, on average are delivered daily. Nearly 200 men are employed and there is besides a large staff of clerks. Messrs. Allman make both Old Pot Still*

*Whiskey, designated Irish and Pure Malt Whiskey, both of a superior
quality, a large trade in which is done in Ireland; their principal
business is, however, with England, Scotland and the Colonies. The
annual output is a little over 500,000 gallons.*"

Once again, as had happened down the centuries of strife in Ireland, the
planted English had taken on the Irish mantle, and the inhabitants of Bandon
were no different. Looking down the list of names of those English settlers
who built the first houses in Bandon-bridge and created the new town, such
names as Giles, Hales, Joyce, Allen, Clarke, Carey, Bernard and Atkins
immediately catch the eye. Who would now call their descendants English?

In 1858, John O'Mahony, a draper in South Main Street was the Fenian
organiser for Bandon. Catholic Emancipation having been achieved - Daniel
O'Connell had once addressed the citizens of Bandon from the balcony of
the Devonshire Arms Hotel - the emphasis of history was turning more from
religious differences to the question of ownership of the land and the Irish
Republican Brotherhood (Fenians) was flourishing. O'Mahony had sworn
many Bandon citizens into the Fenians, amongst them one William Philip
Allen who with Larkin and O'Brien was later hanged in Manchester for the
killing of Sergeant Brett. The Manchester Martyrs will always be
remembered in Bandon town.

As the years lengthened into the 20th century, the tone of the political and
religious persuasion of the Bandon Town Commissioners became more and
more nationalistic emphasising the trend in thinking and feeling of the
citizens of the emerging Bandon. In 1615 one of the first enactments of the
free burgesses of Bandon decreed that "no Papist inhabitants shall be
suffered to dwell within the town." On the same day, it was further decreed
that "hoggs, swyne or pigs must be kept in the owner's backyard." This gave
rise to the odious description of Bandon as "the town where the pigs are
Protestant." The records show. however, that, over the years, the Town
Commissioners passed votes of sympathy on the death of prominent leaders

of the Church and State: Archbishop Croke 1902, Pope Leo XIII 1903, King Edward 1910, O'Donovan Rossa 1915, Lord Mayor Terence MacSweeney 1920, Michael Collins, Arthur Griffith, Cathal Brugha and Harry Boland in 1922. During the Civil War, Major General Sean Hales, TD, a native of Bandon was assassinated in Dublin on the 7th of December 1922. The Italian - made statue standing near Bandon's bridge was erected to his memory in 1930.

Today, Bandon is a thriving, prosperous town, the historic gateway to West Cork, welcoming travellers from all over the world. The days are long gone when it could be said that "Turk, Jew or Atheist may enter here, but no Papist...."

West Cork

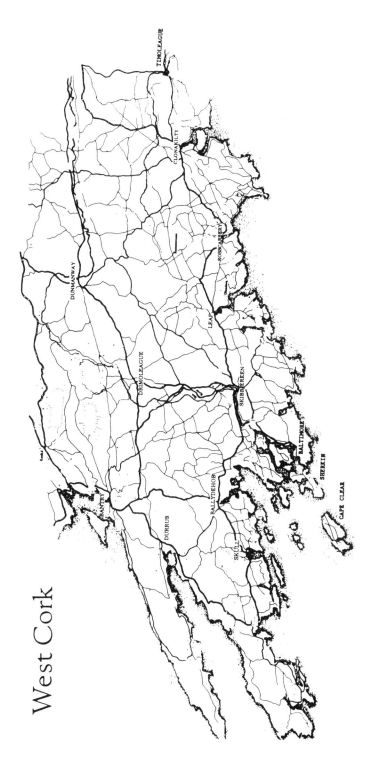

Dunmanway from the Bridge on the Cork Road, 1848.

3

Dunmanway

The name Dunmanway is said to derive from Dun na mBeann mBuide, the fort of the yellow gables or pinnacles, a reference to the profusion of yellow flowered furze bushes which cover the hills overlooking the town. Others claim the derivation comes from Dun na mBan mBuide, the fort of the yellow women. The term "yellow women" referred contemptuously to a garrison of Spanish soldiers because of their long hair and the yellow capes they wore. Like many aspects of history, you may take your pick.

The Castle of Dunmanway was build by Catherine, daughter of Thomas, Earl of Desmond, Lady of Hy-Carbery, "a charitable and truly hospitable woman" who died in 1506. It stood at the western end of the town and was approached by a broad path, now called Castle Road. Unfortunately, there is not even one stone left upon another of this famous old castle, the first stone castle to be erected in this part of Carbery. All its walls were torn down and even its foundations uprooted to furnish building-stone for the erection of a flour-mill which is still in use in nearby Kilbarry.

The long history of Dunmanway is closely interwoven with the colourful career of Sir Richard Cox (1649 - 1733), Lord High Chancellor of Ireland and Speaker of the House of Lords. Those of us born and reared in Dunmanway in the '20s, when history in the making was all around us, may be excused for believing that the career of Sir Richard ended abruptly when he was drowned in the small lake on the outskirts of the town.

After all, famed historian, Daniel Donovan, writing in his **Sketches of Carbery** in 1879, a time much closer to the action, made exactly that mistake. The truth of the matter is that Sir Richard Cox died peacefully in his bed in 1773 at the ripe old age of 84 - it was his great-grandson, Sir Richard Ayre Cox, who came to a watery grave in the lake some fifty years later.

This spoiled, over-rich young Baronet, on hearing that a Wesleyan minister was coming to visit Dunmanway the next day, vowed that he would drag the unwelcome preacher to the nearby lake, half drown him and pack him on his way out of Dunmanway. That evening as he was preparing his boat for the morrow's sport, he fell into the water, hit his head on a stone and was drowned.

The Catholic people of Dunmanway were convinced that the accident happened because Cox had once hit the Catholic priest with his whip. The Protestant people were equally satisfied that God had brought vengeance on the head of the baronet because the oar he used in his boat had been cut from one of the elm trees that grew in the graveyard of the Protestant church. The Wesleyans quite naturally looked on this as a glorious sign from Heaven and a blessing on their missionary work in Dunmanway. In fact, a Methodist Church was established in the town in 1790 and after many enlargements and renovations it still serves the present Methodist population of Dunmanway.

The town owes its existence to the need for a resting - place for troops on the line of march from Bandon to Bantry. Tradition has it that, prior to the building of the fort, the vast tract of country between Dunmanway and Ballineen was covered with dense forest in which many a wayfarer lost his way or fell foul of the outlaws and raparees in his efforts to reach Baltimore or Bantry. In some places the trees were so close together that one might travel seven or eight miles by passing from one tree to the other, Tarzan-like, without once touching the ground.

16

Be that as it may, after the rebellion of 1641, the Dunmanway estates of Teige McCarthy-Downey, which according to the records consisted of *"three ploughlands of Dunmanway, two gneeves of Togher, the west side of Awe, and the western portion of Coolsnarty, in all 2,932 statute acres"* were all bestowed on Colonel William Arnopp, subject to a rent of £22 per annum.

Subsequently, Pierce Arnopp, the Colonel's son, sold the estate to Sir Richard Cox for £1,040. So, to all intents and purposes, the regime of the Cox Family in Dunmanway was now firmly in place and the town had become an English plantation.

Sir Richard, born in Bandon in 1649 and orphaned at the tender age of three, enjoyed a colourful and highly successful life. He was made Recorder of Kinsale in 1673 but fled from Ireland during the reign of James II. He returned to Ireland with William of Orange and for his services at the Battle of the Boyne he was appointed governor of Cork. Now with all his usual bubbling enthusiasm he set about the task of creating a rich and prosperous garrison town in Dunmanway.

Never for a moment doubting the success of his venture, he immediately erected *"a handsome stone bridge of six arches"* over the River Bandon at his own expense. The road out of Dunmanway, across the new bridge and onwards to Bandon, was completed in an amazing six days, although two miles of it ran through bog. In May, 1693 he was granted Letters patent to hold two fairs yearly on April 23rd and November 15th and weekly market on Tuesdays. Thus was Dunmanway officially established.

The town's 300th anniversary was celebrated in 1993 when President Mary Robinson visited Dunmanway and unveiled a plaque in the town Square amid a week of high celebration, pomp and ceremony which the town's founder, Sir Richard Cox would have found entirely fitting.

The original Protestant parish church was in Fanlobbus graveyard about two miles east of the town. One who saw it in 1699 wrote:

"The church is covered but many slates are off. There are no seats or pulpit and about half the church is ruinous."

As his next project, Sir Richard immediately set about building a new church for the Protestant population of his town. When Queen Anne came to the throne in 1702 - he was her first Lord Chancellor - he procured an Act of Parliament by means of which the parish church was to be henceforth in Dunmanway. Accordingly, a church was speedily erected there and dedicated to Saint Mary in honour of his wife, Lady Mary Cox. It was a plain structure and remained in use until 1821 when it was taken down and the present edifice erected on its site at a cost of £1,100. A bargain by any standards!

By the year 1700 there were no less then thirty English families settled in the new town, all of whom Sir Richard reported proudly *"were employed at remunerative work"*.

However, the new town didn't develop as rapidly as he had hoped and, in 1733, according to historian, Charles Smith MD, *"there were not more then 50 very indifferent houses in the town of Dunmanway, 12 not inhabited, or by beggars only, and by 30 people who were for the most part poor and idle for want of employment"*.

Sir Richard Cox died on the 3rd of May 1733, aged 84. Of his seven children, only one son and daughter survived him. His eldest son, Richard, father to Sir Richard Cox, Bart, died in April 15th, 1725. His second and youngest son, Michael was consecrated Lord Bishop of Ossary. All his daughters married and left him many grand-children.

Cox was succeeded by his grandson, Richard and this young man's entrepreneurial drive, inherited no doubt from his illustrious grandfather, soon had the town of Dunmanway humming with a new life. One of his greatest achievements was the introduction of the flax industry to Dunmanway. Realising that agriculture could never sustain the growing population, he energetically introduced this new venture which would give good employment and equally good wages. He bestowed prizes on those who bought and sold the largest quantity of linen manufactured in the town.

Each May-day on the town's fair green he rewarded the girls who excelled at the wheel in the spinning-school. The employer who the previous year had manufactured the best linen, and the greatest quantity of it, had a tablet of honour hung over his door with the inscription in letters of gold, *"Dator Digniori, This house is rent free for the superior industry of the possessor."* The words Dator Digniori, translate from the Latin to: *"Granted to him who is more worthy."* It would appear that as far back as 1750, Sir Richard had introduced what must surely be looked upon as Ireland's very first ISO 9000 Quality Mark.

By 1751 the town boasted a population of 799; of these 410 were Protestants and 389 were Roman Catholics. Sir Richard Cox, the second Baronet, was quite overjoyed as he analysed the figures coming out of the census.

"Blessed by God," he exclaimed, *"there is a decline in the Papist population who in 1749 were 402 and are now down to 389. The Protestants have increased their numbers by five!"*

But because of the contribution that the Cox family had made to the fullness and richness of life in Dunmanway, one should not deny the Baronet his little moment of sectarian exultation.

Some forty years later, in 1793, Sir Richard's successor, Sir John Cox was riding to Cork one Sunday morning when he saw the Catholics of the town kneeling in the rain outside the little thatched cabin they used as a mass-house at the western end of the Long Bridge. *"These are my tenants,"* he thought, *"and it is a shame that they do not have a decent place to worship."* On his return from Cork he sent for the parish priest and offered him a site to build a Catholic Church - the present location - and £20 as a donation to help build the new chapel.

The present church was built by Father Doheny in 1834. He took the innovative course of building the new church around the old building so that finally, with the roof in place, Sunday Mass was said for the last time in the old church. On Monday morning the work of demolishing the old church began and proceeded so well that the new church was ready for the first Mass the following Sunday morning.

To the east of Dunmanway, a distance of about four miles, still stands the ruins of Ballinacarriga Castle built in 1585 by Randal Og Hurley. In its heyday, this castle was a strong, square tower, nearly one hundred feet in height and stood on the crest of a rock which rose upwards of forty feet above the waters of an adjoining lake. A few yards to its front was a small circular tower. This formerly guarded an angle of the wall which enclosed the castle. Unfortunately, the wall and the three other towers at the other angles, were later removed to aid the Dunmanway made a habit of tearing down castles to build flour-mills. On the whole, not a bad habit, perhaps.

The upper floor of the castle contains two large windows, and these are adorned with various illustrations, in relief. On the arch of one is a representation of the Crucifixion, and the Virgin and Child; and on the other, the letters RM.CC (the initials of Randal Murrilah - Hurley - and his wife, Catherine Cullinane), the date of the castle's erection, a ladder, a heart transfixed with crossed swords, a scourge, a cock and a pot. The latter two symbols have always puzzled historians but tradition says that they refer to Peter's denials of Christ in the high priest's courtyard.

Apparently, there was a cock being cooked in a pot on the fire at which Peter stood to warm himself and when Peter denied his Master for the third time the cock jumped out of the boiling water and crowed in his face.

The lot of the stonecutters and masons of Cork was not an easy one. We saw how Lord Cork treated them when the walls of Bandon were being built

20

but Randal Og Hurley of Ballinacarriga treated them even more unfairly when he built his castle.

Ballinacarriga Castle.

Having quarried the stone and collected the other materials necessary for getting the work started, he sent in every direction for stonecutters and masons but they were unwilling to go to such a remote area in the wilds of Carbery. Nothing could coax them but big money and Randal readily promised them wages way above the going rate. He had cabins erected for their accommodation, fed them the best oxen and pig meat and they, in turn, worked hard and with cheerful good-will. Occasionally a married man drew some of his wages to send home to his family, but the great bulk of what was due to the workers was left untouched. They looked forward with pleasure to the vast sums that would be theirs on the completion of the castle. It was a happy building site.

At last, the day arrived when the castle was completed and Randal announced that he would give a great feast to celebrate the occasion. Not only were all the workmen invited, but also the tenants and gallow-glasses belonging to himself and his kindred. After they had all enjoyed a bountiful meal, washed down with large measures of Spanish wine, Randal invited his guests to join him outside the walls for further entertainment. They followed him out in excellent humour and he then ordered the gates to be closed and the gallow-glasses to be drawn up under arms. Calling the workmen, one by one, he ordered them to produce their tally-sticks so that he could pay what he owed. As each man produced his stick, Randal produced a set-off in the shape of board and lodgings and many of them, he claimed, were actually in his debt.

He then ordered them off his lands and warned that if any of them were caught near his castle after nightfall they would be executed. By sun-rise they had put as much distance as possible between themselves and Ballinacarriga's castle, leaving their curses for ever on the Hurleys of West Carbery.

Life at the castle was vigorous and exciting. While her lord was at the chase, Lady Randal would supervise the details for many great banquets. She was an imperious woman yet the people held her in high esteem.

One night there came a knocking at the castle gates. Lady Randal was close by and it was she who answered. *"Who comes at this time of night?"* she asked haughtily.

A feeble voice came from the darkness: *"Tis I, a poor beggar woman, my lady, craving for a rest for the night, and a little something to eat."*

Lady Randal shivered contemptuously. *"A rest? And food? Begone, woman, and quickly. There is no rest or food here for the likes of you"*

Then the beggar-woman spoke again. *"But, your ladyship, I have seven children and they are hungry...."*

Lady Randal's voice became disdainful . *"Seven children,"* she shrilled. *"And whose fault is that? Not mine, I can assure you. Begone, I say!"*

There was a faint rustle in the night as the woman gathered her children about her. Then she spoke again: *"Go I shall, my lady, but before I do, listen to what I say, You are, I know, expecting your first child. But when it is born, six others will you have, making as many as I have altogether."*

Months later when Randal Og was returning from a hunt, he met the castle washerwoman making her way towards the lake. It seemed to him that her basket was unusually heavy. He reined in his horse. *"What have you in that basket?"* he demanded.

The washerwoman curtsied. *"Nothing, your honour, nothing but a few pups I was going to drown in the lake."*

Lord Randal dismounted. *"Who dares sends any pups of mine to be drowned?"* he stormed. He snatched at the basket's cover. And there curled up in what might have been their last sleep were six baby boys. *"What is the meaning of this?"* he demanded. *"Tell me all or forfeit your ancient head within the next few seconds."*

Life was sweet even to the old washerwoman, so tremblingly she told Randal Og of the beggar woman's visit and the curse she put on Lady Randal when help was refused. *"Only this morning, your honour, and you but hardly gone to the chase, were the children born. One was kept and I was told to drown the others. What could I do but obey?"*

Randal was silent for a few moments. His followers watched, wondering what was going to happen. At last Randal spoke: *"Yes, woman, there was nothing you could do. But now you must keep silence, all of you, silence for seven years. The least talk of this matter and a head will be forfeited."*

So it was arranged. There and then, six nurses, all sworn to secrecy were obtained for the six babies. Lord Randal returned to the castle. He was told the good news that his wife had borne him a son. He dashed up the stairs to congratulate her but not the slightest sign did he show that he knew anything of the curse of the beggar woman and its result.

Seven years passed and, as was customary, Randal Og Hurley ordered a great banquet to be held in honour of his son's seventh birthday. The guests were seated and waited for the boy to make his ceremonial entrance.

Lady Randal was in her place at the head of the table. Suddenly she noticed that there were six vacant seats alongside that set for her son. She had hardly time to think why this was so when in came not one boy but seven, all similarly dressed. They walked slowly towards her. The blood drained from her cheeks. Her brain reeled. What was this? Had the six children come back as ghosts from the bottom of the lake? How could this be? She fainted.

For long minutes there was pandemonium in the Banqueting Hall. Lady Randal was revived, hardly knowing what was going on. Her husband placed an affectionate arm about her and raised his hand for silence. He then told the guests the whole story, leaving nothing out.

"Let it be a warning," he said in conclusion, *"never to refuse a poor person either food or shelter or both. We are all God's creatures - the rich and the poor, and the lowly."*

Today, 400 years on, Randal Hurley's remains lie in nearby Fanlobbus graveyard. The towering ruins of his castle just a few miles away still bravely defy the ravages of time and weather.

Randal Og's seven sons, with their father's enthusiasm and bravery, joined hopefully with the rebel Irish forces in the rebellion of 1641 and paid dearly the penalty for defeat. The castle, lands and cattle were declared forfeit and the Hurleys of Ballinacarriga remained hunted outlaws till they died. So perhaps the curse of the stonemasons of Cork did catch up with them after all.

No look back at the Dunmanway of the 1600's would be complete without reference to the famed yew tree that has given the hills to the north of the town their name. A historian of the period, Bennett of Bandon, - his leanings were to the Ascendancy class if one is to judge by the tone of his account - had this to say:

"On the summit of the Yew Tree mountain once stood a famous tree. It was a tall and gracious specimen of old Irish yew: and its bulk was such that, at a distance of two yards from the ground, it had a circumference of no less than eighteen feet. This venerable tree, amongst whose branches the sunlight played when a McCarthy sat on the throne of Cork, was ruthlessly cut down by the Irishry and hacked into planks of about seven feet to be hawked around Dunmanway for firewood. One of these pieces was rescued by a Protestant gentleman from the degradation of heating the shins of some Dunmanway barbarian and he made a handsome bedstead of it; but all the rest experienced the fate intended for the whole - chopped up into blocks and stuck under pots to boil potatoes and heat the houses..."

By May, 1747, according to historian Charles Smith, there were 87 houses in Dunmanway, which contained 250 Protestants and 307 Catholics. At that time, there were reckoned to be 87 flax wheels and 51 woollen wheels operating in the growing town. In May, 1749, the number of houses had increased to 117, containing 405 Protestants and 402 Catholics. There were now 226 flax wheels operating in the town but the number of woollen wheels had decreased to a mere 28, besides those in the spinning-school.

Richard Pococke who visited Dunmanway around 1758 wrote:

"The town consists of one street and some houses built for weavers by Sir Richard Cox and a bridge over the river which leads to a Green beautifully planted on each side of which are the houses of labourers and others, and a quarter of a mile to the east, a bleach yard. There are about 60 looms and spinning goes on sufficient for them. It is a most

agreeable sight to see children employed in reeling even from four years old and such a general face of industry."

Whether modern trade union leaders would be as delighted as Mr. Pococke to behold such agreeable work practices is highly debatable, In 1800 Mr. John Atkins built a tannery in River Lane, later called Tanyard Lane, and brought much prosperity to the area. The tannery produced excellent leather for boot-making and harness-making, both of which industries flourished in the town. By 1810 Dunmanway had two tanyards as well as two mills capable of grinding annually 15,000 bags of flour, A porter and ale brewery established in 1831 produced 23,600 barrels of porter annually.

"Several new roads have been recently opened leading to the town," reported a traveller of the period, *"and a fine and level line leads from Cork to Bantry."*

Referring to the thriving industry of the town, Charles Smith had this to say:

"Happy would it be for many parts of this country if, instead of that spirit of devastation which dairies produce, our villages were thus filled with manufactures, who ought to be supported and encouraged in this manner by an indulgent landlord which would, in the end, produce honour and wealth to him and his dependants."

Smith's words could be looked upon as almost prophetic when the dread blight of famine stalked the land in the late 1840's . Dunmanway, unfortunately, did not fully escape the ravages of famine and famine graves may still be seen in Fanlobbus graveyard. However, unlike other towns in West Cork, Skibbereen and Clonakilty especially, because the people of Dunmanway depended more on the town's industries than on agriculture, the dread famine was kept at bay. For example, when the numbers of inmates in Bantry Workhouse was reported to be 2,327 persons and 600 children at the height of the Great Famine, Dunmanway Workhouse reached its maximum occupation of just 443 in July, 1847.

The long war for independence from England reached out to Dunmanway in November 1920, when a convoy of Black and Tans en route from Macroom to Dunmanway was ambushed at Kilmichael to the north of the town by a group of Irish Volunteers under the command of General Tom Barry. Eighteen British soldiers and three Irish were killed and The Boys of Kilmichael had marched gloriously into Irish song and history. Unfortunately, just a month later in December, 1920, the Tans took their revenge by murdering the town's Parish Priest, Canon Magnier and a passer-by, Dan Crowley just a mile or so east of the town. A monument was erected at the place of the murder in 1921.

Sectarianism has never been seen as a problem in Dunmanway. Unlike Lord Cork in Bandon who in a letter to Lord Goring, dated January 6th, 1642, stated,

"I thank God I have planted the town of Bandon that there is neither an Irishman nor a Papist within the walls..."

Sir Richard Cox, on the other hand, had always insisted that Catholic and Protestant should be allowed to live side by side in his town. However, to Dunmanway's shame, sectarianism did surface in 1922 when three highly respected Protestant townspeople, Mr. Fitzmaurice of Carbery House, Mr. Grey of Sackville Street, and his neighbour, Mr. Buttimer, an elderly, blind man who had to be helped by his wife to come down from his bedroom, were all murdered in cold blood at their own front doors.

A resident of the town who witnessed part of the incident had this to tell:

"The murders were carried out by members of the local anti-treaty forces who had occupied the empty RIC barracks in Main Street, They appeared to be extremely drunk and the plot to murder the Protestants was hatched out in a local pub in retaliation for what was going on in

Belfast at the time when Catholics were, allegedly, being murdered by Protestants. Strangely, the flag outside the barracks was flown at half mast next day, signalling, one hopes, that the dastardly deed carried out in the drunken anger of night was deeply regretted in the sober light of day..."

Fair Day in Dunmanway, 1890 - 1900.

Subsequently, some Protestant families, to the genuine regret of their Catholic neighbours, left Dunmanway and settled in Northern Ireland.

Sam Maguire, a member of a distinguished Protestant farming family and whose name is inscribed on Gaelic Football's most prized trophy, was born in 1879 at Mallabracka about three miles north of Dunmanway. At the age of twenty years he, like Michael Collins, was appointed to the British Civil Service and worked in London. Whilst there, he held many official positions in the London GAA, including chairmanship of the London County Board. During the struggle for independence he became Lieutenant General in the

IRA and Director of Intelligence in Britain. After the Treaty he returned to Ireland but soon found himself out of favour with the political authorities in Dublin and was relieved of all his responsibilities. He returned, dispirited, to his beloved Dunmanway farm where he died. He was buried in the graveyard in St. Mary's Church, and the family home is now a Memorial Park.

Subsequently, the All-Ireland Football Trophy, the Sam Maguire Cup, was presented to the GAA as a lasting memorial to this great Protestant patriot from Dunmanway.

Nowadays, the economic success and prosperity of Dunmanway is bound up inexorably with that of the West Cork farmer, coupled with the varied industries located in the thriving Industrial Estate at Underhill. The Cox Memorial Hall, erected in the 1800's by the Protestant population of Dunmanway to the memory of the town's distinguished founder, Sir Richard Cox, is now, appropriately perhaps, incorporated in a thriving supermarket in the town's main street. This supermarket, part of the Centra Group, is owned by Mr. Robert Kingston whose family has farmed in the Dunmanway area for many generations. Sir Richard would have approved of that.

Without doubt, Dunmanway went through hard times in the nineteenth and early twentieth century when emigration bled the town of its youth and vigour, but those times are now, hopefully, gone for ever.

4

Ballineen / Enniskeane

Some eight miles east of Dunmanway lie the twin villages of Ballineen and Enniskeane. Writing of Ballineen in the 1800's, Historian Bennett said that *"Ballineen consists of one long street running east and west, and of another street starting from its centre and running due south to the Bandon River. At one time it belonged to the Earls of Cork but was later purchased by the late Lord Bandon and since then it has been almost rebuilt."*

"Some years ago this large district enjoyed a very unenviable notoriety. The pernicious practice of illicit distillation was openly carried on there to a great extent; and we regret to say, murder was not of unfrequent occurrence also. But since it has passed into the hands of the late Earl, a great change has been effected for the better. Those amongst whom were many who spent their time in unlawful pursuits, and many at whose door grave charges were laid, were removed, and their places filled by an industrious, orderly and contented tenentry...."

Today, the proud tenentry of Ballineen stand tall in their picturesque village which has spread eastwards to join up with the neighbouring village of Enniskeane. At the western end, Carbery Milk Products, Ltd., provides gainful employment for the workers of this area. And, whatever about the illicit distillation of long ago, which so shocked Historian Bennett, a high class alcohol is now quite lawfully distilled at Carbery Milk Products and, with all its other products, marketed successfully throughout Europe.

To the north of Enniskeane stands the celebrated Kinneigh Round Tower. It is an unusual structure, being hexagonal in form from the base to a height of eighteen feet, and circular from that up. The tower formally had a conical roof but this was altered by an unknown vandal cleric to allow for its use as a bell tower. This unique tower is the only one of its type in Ireland. Smith in his Ancient Monuments of the County and City of Cork has this to say about Kinneigh:

Kinneigh Tower, north of Enniskeane.

"Kinneth steeple is six storeys high, each eleven feet, nine inches and is different from all other round towers I have heard about. The first storey is a regular hexagon, each being ten foot four inches; from this storey it is to the top quite round, being in the whole seventy feet four inches high. It stands one hundred and twenty-four feet from the west end of the ruined church and it is remarkable that the doors of most of these towers face the west entrance of the church or churchyards..."

Every Irish child going to school is taught that round towers were built to protect the ancient monks from the marauding Danes. At the first sign of danger they betook themselves with their treasures within the tower, there to remain in safety till the danger was past. Smith offers a different theory:

"The Irish name for a penance," he writes, "is Turris, i.e. the latin name for a tower, derived from penitents being imprisoned in them. And it is no less certain that most of the Irish ecclesiastical words are directly taken from Latin, as Temple, Aglish, Ashbeg, etc., from Templum, Ecclesia, Episcopus, etc. Penitents were placed in the top of the tower, and having made a probation of a particular number of days according to their crime, they were admitted to descend to the next floor and so on, till they came to the door which always faced the entrance of the church, were they stood and received the absolution of the clergy and the blessings of the people."

Dr. Smith's theory offers a much more acceptable picture than the unedifying spectacle of portly monks scrambling in terror up rickety ladders with a couple of gold chalices under one arm and the Book of Kells, or whatever, under the other.

In an ancient Irish MS., containing some annals of Munster, there is mention made of the building of this tower at Kinneagh about the year 1015, soon after the Battle of Clontarf when Brian Boru defeated the Danes.

This manuscript states that

"Cian or Kean, being married to the eldest daughter of Brian, late monarch of Ireland, set about conquering the Kingdom from Donnel, the lawful heir, who was his brother-in-law. The second daughter of Brian was married to Donnel who marched with 1,000 men near this tower of Kinneagh, then building and almost finished by St. Mocholomog the patron thereof, and implored the saint's blessing, which he received."

"Cian being in pursuit of Donnel came up to Kinneagh with 3,000 men, suffered them to plunder it, and carry away the provisions of the workmen, for which he and his army were cursed by the saint, and coming up with Donnel, were overthrown by him at a place called Ballingully, now Mogolin, six miles west of Cork."

Once again, history and historians offer a variety of views of the same picture to you, the reader, to pick the one of your choice. And if Smith has his dates right, Kinneigh Round Tower has imprisoned penitents and withstood the onslaught of time, weather and marauding armies for close on a thousand years...

5

Macroom

Macroom - the plain of Crom - was formerly spelt Macromp. Smith, in his **History of Cork**, says *"the town takes its name from an old crooked tree which grew to an enormous size and stood there a long time, and under the branches of which travellers used to rest themselves."* No doubt, as modern travellers' halting sites quickly develop into sprawling townships in their own right, a similar development happened under this famous tree.

It has also been suggested that the terms Corna, Crom or Cruach refer to some obscure deity of pagan times. After Druidism disappeared, the bards, who were next in importance to the first Order of the Pagan Priesthood retained most of the privileges they had previously possessed. For centuries after the introduction of Christianity they continued to hold their assemblies here on the plain of Crom.

Various historical opinions seem to agree that a castle was built here in the year 1100 by the Carew Clan on the site of an earlier stronghold of the O'Flyns. The town probably grew around the castle and it had some new blood poured into it when Cormac McCarthy in the reign of James the First, induced the Hardings, Kents, Goolds, Fields and other English families to settle there.

In 1641, Donagh, Lord Muskerry, who lived in Macroom Castle, was one of the most prominent leaders in the great rebellion. Upon its suppression in 1652, the town, castle and the vast territorial estates of that nobleman were forfeited. Upon the accession of Charles the Second, however, they were restored, and enjoyed by his descendants until the reign of William the Third, when they were again forfeited because of the active part taken by Donagh, the fourth Earl of Clancarthy in the cause of James the Second.

Macroom Castle and Bridge.

Pigot's diary of 1824 describes Macroom as follows:

"A market, post and fair town in Cork. Pleasantly situated on the River Sullane and from the proximity of bog and mountain is well supplied with turf. It has a weekly market and some respectable dwelling houses. The County Sessions are held there. Robert Eyre resides in the castle which has been lately repaired and furnished in a style of elegance and taste. The venerable and stately building, the front of which is covered with ivy is said to have been build 700 years ago...."

In 1602 the castle's then owner, Cormac Mac Dermot Carthy (Lord Muskerry) was suspected of treason and taken to prison in Cork. At that time Sir Charles Wilmot laid siege to the castle to plant the English flag there for ever, but all his efforts to break the will of the occupying McCarthy clan were in vain. After a long and frustrating siege he made up his mind to strike his tents and abandon the enterprise altogether. Fortune smiled on him that night.

Macroom Castle from Market Square.

Historian George Bennett gives this graphic description of the unfortunate fall of the castle to Wilmot's forces:

"It appears that the castle warders were sadly in want of fresh provisions so they decided to kill a pig. No-one, even in those rude times, could think of eating the meat with the bristles on. What to do? They had no spare water to scald them off as Wilmot's men held tight

control over the River Sullane which flowed nearby. So, why not use some of the straw and fern upon which they slept, and singe it off!"

"The dead porker is raised on end and is surrounded with the combustibles just mentioned, a light is applied and the martyr to their anxiety for fresh meat is circled with flames.....They would seem, at all events, to have been making merry in some way, and not to mind what they were about, as they suffered some of the lighted straw to fall on the thatched roof of a cabin which lay against the wall of the bawn outside. The roof instantly blazed up, and the flash bounding through an open window seized on a loft of tallow and other ignitables. Thus vigorously sustained, the giant blaze whirled and roared as it rushed along, filled every apartment, and soon the whole castle was lapped in flames."

The McCarthys were terrified. With no water to fight the conflagration, they were forced to flee the castle. In their efforts many did escape, but about fifty were overtaken and killed.

When Wilmot's forces entered the castle, and having command of the waters of the River Sullane, they quickly extinguished the flames and Macroom castle was taken. Sir Charles laid in a supply of provisions, barracked a company of foot there, and set out for Cork.

When Lord Muskerry was eventually released from prison, he had the castle restored. In 1650 Lord Broghill of Bandon, who was dispatched from Clonmel by Cromwell, marched on Macroom. The garrison of the castle, aware of his approach, joined the main Irish body which lay encamped in the park. Broghill immediately attacked and the Irish army, outnumbered and outgunned, broke and fled, leaving a great many dead. Several prisoners were taken, amongst whom was the Bishop of Ross, Boetius McEgan.

Lord Broghill took the Bishop to Carrigadrohid Castle and offered him his life if he would induce the garrison there to lay down their arms. The Bishop accepted Broghill's terms but when brought within talking distance of the castle he told the garrison to hold out to the last man. Broghill ordered a gallows to be erected forthwith and the bishop was hanged on the spot.

Cromwell never forgave the people of Macroom for their stout resistance to his rule and when his son-in-law, General Ireton was made Lord President of Ireland, he sent some troops from Kilkenny, who burned not only the castle but the town as well. The ruins of the castle were presented to William Penn who restored it and lived in it for a short time. His son William was the founder of the State of Pennsylvania, USA. Eventually, ownership of the castle reverted to the McCarthys. When once again the McCarthys were found guilty of treason for siding with King James, the castle came into the possession of Judge Bernard of Bandon, an ancestor of the Earl of Bandon.

The Honourable Judge Bernard of Castle Bernard.

In addition to the fairs which were held in Macroom when he became the owner, the judge obtained a patent, dated September 3rd, 1712, for holding four more, namely, on the 1st of May, on July 1st, September 1st, and on the 1st of November; and two markets, one to be held on Wednesday, and one on Saturday.

In 1891 the castle was acquired by Olive White, a member of the White family of Bantry House. Olive, known as Lady Ardilaun, was married to Arthur Guinness of Dublin. For his charity and generosity to the people of Dublin, Mr. Guinness was given the title Baron Ardilaun.

Once again, as had happened at least four times in its long history, the castle was burnt by Anti-Treaty forces in the Civil War of 1922-23. Lady Ardilaun then sold the Castle Demesne to a group of Macroom businessmen to be held in trust for the people of Macroom for ever. At the time, she retained the castle for sentimental reasons. However, by 1966, the castle was in such a dangerous state of repair that it had to be demolished. Bishop McEgan College now stands on the site of the castle and the Demesne contains a football pitch, a golf course and riverside walks.

Unfortunately, the facade of the castle is all that remains now, but the grounds are open to the public. The public library is situated in the walls by the entrance to the gates. Here, in the 40's, the building was, in fact, the local cinema. Where nowadays two magnificent cannons stand guard outside the gates of Macroom Castle, there then stood a large billboard proclaiming the joys to be experienced that night by watching the latest epic of Earl Flynn and Jean Harlow or Clarke Gable and Myrna Loy. Whatever about the quality of the entertainment provided inside, the entrance to the Macroom Cinema must have been the most historically picturesque in the world. Macroom Castle has had a long and exciting history.

Today, Macroom is a bustling market town and a popular half-way stopping point for tourists heading from Cork to Killarney. With what remains of its historic castle, its graceful square usually bustling in open market, an imposing Town Hall, beautiful parks and walks, Macroom looks not just to its historic past, but to a highly successful future.

Timoleague Abbey.

6

Timoleague and Courtmacsherry

imoleague, formerly spelt Tagumlag, Tymulagy or Tymoleague, derives its name from Tig Molaga (the house of Molaga), an Irish saint who lived in 665 A.D., and to whom the abbey, built in the beginning of the fourteenth century was dedicated. St. Molaga was a native of Fermoy and his principal monastery there was called Tulach-Min Molaga. His feast day was on the 20th January. It is not known when he died but he was alive in 665 AD having survived the great plague which raged in that year.

The town of Timoleague, and most of the adjoining countryside, belonged to the Hodnetts, an English family who came to Ireland from Shropshire. According to Charles Smith,

"the family degenerated into the Irish customs and assumed the name of McSherry from whence came the name of the village of Courtmacsherry."

In the reign of Henry the Third, (1216 - 1272) a battle was fought at Timoleague between the Hodnetts, under Lord Philip Hodnett, and the Barrys, under Lord Barrymore. The Hodnetts were routed and Lord Philip was killed. The Barrymores and their descendants then became the Lords of Timoleague and Courtmacsherry.

In 1589, in the reign of Elizabeth, Timoleague was well known as a seaport town, and in that year was mentioned in documents, in conjunction with Kinsale, as being *"market and haven towns, the furthest not a myle from the maine sea."* In fact, long before Bandon was founded, Timoleague was a thriving town containing more than a dozen hostelries where Irish gentlemen and Spanish merchants would rest and regale themselves with a stimulating glass or two of the best of Spanish wines. Afterwards, the merchants betook themselves to the town's market-place and bartered their wines and olives for the hides and butter for which Timoleague was justly famous even as far afield as Spain.

Timoleague Abbey was built in 1320 by Daniel McCarthy, prince of Carbery. It is stated that the ground upon which it was erected was previously occupied by a building erected by the Morils in 1206 and taken from them by the McCarthys. In 1373, William Barry, Lord of Ibane, was buried there. In 1400 it was given to the Franciscans Order. Edmund de Courcey added a handsome Gothic tower which stood seventy feet high and is still in good repair today. De Courcey had been a monk in Timoleague Abbey and was subsequently raised to the See of Clogher. He was the first prelate of English descent that ever wore the mitre in that diocese. He died in March, 1518, at a very advanced age and was buried in his beloved abbey.

A Father Mooney, Provincial of the Irish Franciscans, visited the abbey in 1603 and wrote:

"The church was indeed a splendid edifice, having a spacious choir, aisle, lateral wing and magnificent tall tower. The cloister was very beautiful, square, richly arcaded and covered with a platform, on which was a suite of apartments, comprising chapter-room, refectory, and the guardians' ample chamber. Along with these, the convent had also its dormitory, kitchen, cellars and other appurtenances which made it one of the noblest houses of our Order in Ireland. When I visited the place, the entire edifice was still standing, though sadly in need of being repaired; for indeed it has suffered much from the ruthless vandalism of the English soldiers, and also from the sacrilegious rapacity of William

Lyons, Protestant Bishop of Cork, and a certain Doctor Hamner, an Anglican minister."

"During the later war, a body of English soldiers, consisting of one hundred of infantry and fifty horsemen, halted before Timoleague and, entering the church, began to smash the beautiful stained-glass windows, and destroy the various pictures above the altar. It so happened that the carpenter, whom our friars employed to look after the repairs of the sacred edifice, was present on this occasion; and seeing the impiety of those creedless mercenaries, he addressed himself to our holy founder thus: 'St. Francis, in whose honour this house was built, I know that thou art all-powerful with God, and canst obtain from him whatever thou ask. Now, I solemnly swear that I will never do another day's work in this monastery, if thou dost not take speedy vengeance on these sacrilegious wretches who have destroyed the holy place."

"And, indeed, it would appear that the poor man's prayers were speedily answered; for on the following day, when the soldiers had struck their tents, after doing such serious damage to the church and monastery, they were encountered by Daniel O'Sullivan, Prince of Beare, who, with a small force under his command, fell upon them and cut them to pieces. Dr. Hamner, whom I previously mentioned, destroyed the dormitory in 1596; for he came in a small vessel to Timoleague, in order to procure timber for a house he was building near Cork; and having learnt that the friars' cells were wainscoted with oak elaborately carved, he pulled asunder the rich woodwork, and placed it aboard his vessel. But his sacrilege was duly avenged; for his ship had hardly put to sea, when a gale sprang up and sent it with its freight to the bottom. Lyons, the Protestant bishop of Cork, was an unrelenting enemy to our convent of Timoleague, and never spared that beautiful house when he required building materials. In 1590, having commenced building a mill, he and his posse made a descent on a mill

*belonging to our friars, which stood on the Arrighideen, and carried off
the hammer-stones and machinery; which he re-erected in his own
neighbourhood. Soon afterwards, however, an inundation swept away
all his work; and many who witnessed the fact attributed it to the
indignation of Heaven"*

Let those, then, who would learn from the lessons of history, forever
beware the curse of the simple carpenters of Timoleague. Like their
colleague, the Carpenter of far-off Nazareth, they would appear to be well
connected to people in High Places.

In the beautiful city of Prague, capital of the Czech Republic, the Jewish
cemetery has become a tourist attraction which draws thousands of visitors
every year. In its day, it was a small cemetery and when there was no more
room in it to inter the bodies of the dead Jews of Prague, their astute
relatives found a simple if unusual solution to their problem. They placed the
corpses of their loved ones on top of the ground and covered them over with
a layer of earth. Consequently, the ground-level of the cemetery is now ten
feet higher than the surrounding streets.

A similar problem arose in Timoleague abbey. Such had been the desire
of the native people to be buried within its sacred precincts, that on several
occasions the bones of many who had been interred there had been removed
to make room for fresh arrivals. Unlike the Jews of Prague, the Irish solution
to this Irish problem was much more pragmatic. Writing in 1869, the
Bandon historian, George Bennett, who had visited the abbey about that time
said:

*"All these bones and skulls were collected, and arranged in the form
of a wall; and up to about twenty-five years ago, they were the first to
catch the visitor's attention on his arrival at the grave-yard. At present,
the lower portion of this crumbling structure can still be seen, but it is
so overgrown with moss as to escape the eye of the ordinary observer.
The building itself is in very fair condition. For this it is soley indebted*

to the late Colonel Travers, who, at considerable expense, repaired and strengthened the walls, and by these and other means kept them from falling. So that to this gentleman it is owning that a feature prominent in the landscape for over five hundred years is yet in being, and the student and tourist can still visit and admire the venerable abbey of Timoleague."

The story of the wall of skulls is confirmed in an article in the November 1st 1834 issue of the Dublin Penny Journal. The writer says: *"In one of the aisles there is a wall of skulls, about four feet high, and ten feet long, which the people hold sacred."*

One can only hope and pray that when the good Colonel Travers met his end, there was room in the cemetery to accept his remains. But not withstanding the fame that this old abbey had brought to Timoleague over the centuries when it was a beacon light for saints and scholars from all over Europe, there is a sad and inglorious episode in the town's history which must be put on record. It gives no pleasure to do so.

Around about the year 1840, a new master was appointed to the National School in Timoleague. In order to ingratiate himself with his pupils and generate a good feeling in the school to the new master, he gave the pupils a half-holiday. The playground at that time was the abbey and graveyard. Boys being boys, the happy band raced through the ruins, some exploring the vaults which contained the remains of several of the descendants of the champions of England in the reign of King John. Others scaled the high walls and raced one another around the dangerous summits. The heavy boot of one boy struck off a flag and it gave out a hollow sound. Calling two of his companions to help him, he set about lifting the heavy slab. Dreams of golden chalices and other treasures hidden away by the monks spurred on their efforts. Finally they succeeded in raising up the guarding stone but instead of gold goblets and glittering treasure all that was revealed was an old parchment book.

In their disappointment, they hurled the musty volume down into the nave below where the rest of their companions used it as a football, kicking it from one end of the abbey to the other and back again. Tiring of their game, they threw the battered book into a nearby pool and stoned it to keep it under the water. There was, unfortunately, worse to come. When the boys had departed, a herd of pigs arrived and proceed to eat the precious manuscript page by page as they ripped the volume to shreds.

When the schoolmaster heard of the episode that evening, he hurried to the abbey but, to his great distress, all he found was a tattered remnant of what once had been the cover. Thus ingloriously perished a manuscript which would have been as welcome and invaluable to the students of Irish history as the Annals of the Four Masters. It was, in fact, to Timoleague that the writers of the Annals came when they were writing the history of Ireland in the early 17th century, for the abbey's library was known to contain records of much of the early history of the area. The Book of Timoleague, had it survived, would surely have ranked proudly beside the Book of Kells. Unthinking vandalism is not a new plague visited upon the people of Ireland during the 20th century. Unfortunately, it has been with us always.

The article in the Dublin Penny Journal, referred to earlier, suggests that the original site for the Abbey was about a mile from Timoleague on the Clonakilty road.

"But," says the writer, *"the work that was done during the day always fell at night - no doubt shaken from the foundations by the strong arm of the good people whose fort already occupied this place."* Legend has it that the a new site was chosen by releasing a sheaf of wheat with a lighted candle placed upon it onto the river Argideen, and having floated downstream, it came ashore at a point where the abbey was then built.

Today, under the towering beauty of the abbey's well-preserved walls, the village of Timoleague nestles picturesquely at the water's edge at the head of a long sea inlet in West Cork's Gulf Stream Coast. It, like the nearby village, Courtmacsherry, is a quiet, peaceful haven for the visiting tourist and historian in search of the past. Ballymore Castle Gardens, just outside the village, are open to the public. Picnic grounds and a children's playground are laid out among palm trees and other exotic shrubs bringing a touch of subtropical splendour to this historic old village.

Timoleague's glory, however, is in its past; its peace and tranquillity is in the present. The saintly spirit of Saint Molaga lingers on....

7

Rosscarbery

osscarbery or, anciently, Ross-Alithir (the wood of the pilgrims) was conferred by Henry the Second on Robert Fitz-Stephen and Miles de Cogan in 1170 after the Norman invasion. These Norman knights, in turn, bestowed the town and all the lands of Ross, (*"save those belonging to the Bishop"*) upon Adam de Roche. Subsequently, a charter of incorporation, by which many privileges were secured to *"Ross Lehir,"* was granted to the town by King John, circa 1199.

Like most cathedral towns, the cathedral or abbey was first erected and then a town soon nestled beneath its walls. Such was the origin of Rosscarbery.

Says Dr. Hamner, in his **Chronicles of Ireland,** published in 1571 - the same Dr. Hamner, by the way, who so wantonly desecrated the Abbey of Timoleague and made off with the elaborately carved oak wainscoting from the monks' dormitory:

"At the beginning of the sixth century, St. Faghna or Fachna lived in the time of Finbarr and founded a monastery upon the sea, in the south part of Ireland, where he became abbot; and which seat grew to be a city, wherin a cathedral church was built and patronized by Faghna. This town, of old called Ross Lithry, but now Roskarbry, hath been walled about by a lady of that county; but now according to the fruits of war among the Carties, O'Driscoles, and other septs, scarce can the old foundations be seen. There hath been there of old a great University,

whereto resorted all the south-west part of Ireland, for learning sake. St. Brendan, Bishop of Kerry, read publicly the liberal sciences in that school."

In 979 A.D. the town was pillaged by marauding Danes but little is known of the extent of the damage inflicted on the fledgling community. That they survived, however, is evident because they were flourishing again on the arrival of the Normans in the 12th century..

A little known fact, even in West Cork, is that the first Christians in Ireland were the Corcaliaghde of Carbery, who were believers in Christ long before the arrival of Saint Patrick. From their line sprang a saintly matron, Liedania, the mother of Saint Kiernan, born on the Island of Cape Clear, 352 AD. From the Corcailaighde line also came Mongach The Hairy; (so called because he was born with hair). St. Fachtna, the founder of Rosscarbery Abbey, was the son of Mongach.

Archbishop Usher speaks very highly of the renowned school of Ross-Alithir and states that *"a city grew up there owing to the great influx of students from all parts."*

There is a legend about St. Fachtna, the patron saint of Ross, which says that it was his pious custom to pray daily on the side of a hill, half a mile to the east of Ross. One day, in an unusual moment of forgetfulness, he left his prayer- book behind him and the following night turned out to be very wet and stormy. Nevertheless, says the legend, not a drop of rain touched the holy book as the angels, knowing that the rain was coming, hurried down from Heaven and build a chapel over the book to protect it.

Dr. Charles Smith in his **History of Cork,** published in 1815, refers thus to the angels' chapel:

"This chapel was, about 50 years ago, repaired by a resident of Rosscarbery, who, in a fit of sickness, had vowed, if he recovered, to build a church, and he fixed on this spot to fulfil his vow,"

Historian Gibson, in his **History of Cork,** referring to the same incident, remarks rather uncharitably:

"To build a church and rebuild an oratory are different things. This parsimonious penitent of Rosscarbery built on the old foundations of the little oratory which were but twelve feet long and eight feet broad. Probably he may have pleaded the sacredness of the spot, and that he built on the foundations of the angles, for religion is often pleaded as a cloak of covetousness. When the devil is sick, the devil a saint will be...."

Nevertheless, however parsimonious the sick gentleman of Rosscarbery may or may not have been, the walls of the church he built in honour of Saint Fachtna are still there on the hill east of Ross and are prayerfully viewed by the thousands of tourists who pass through the village every year. Locally, the ruined oratory is called Templefaughnan, or The Little Church of Saint Fachtna.

St . Fachtna was succeeded by St. Finchad, who was a pupil of St. Finbarr's. He was followed, down the years, by twenty-four bishops, all of the same family line, but, unfortunately, not one of their names had been preserved till the arrival of Dongal Mac Folact, the twenty-seventh Bishop. An extract from the ancient Book of Lechan glorifies this event in Latin, which translated to English, reads:

"Hail, happy Ross, that could produce thrice nine -

All mitred sages of Liedanias line.

From Fachnan, crowned with everlasting praise,

Down to the date of Donga's pious days."

When the Normans arrived in this area the Benedictine monks founded a priory on the south side of the town. To the east of this stood the original St. Fachna's Cathedral. The Cathedral, which had always been used as a parish church, was demolished and rebuilt as a Protestant Cathedral in 1612. It was regarded as one of the most handsome buildings of its era and had a square tower.

Subsequent alterations and additions in the 18th century have left us today with an equally handsome building of which the spire is probably the only part of the original design. The cathedral is still in use to this day, half being a museum, the other half a place of worship.

A writer of the time had this to tell:

"It was in a vault in this building - which was taken down and rebuilt some years ago - that Mrs. Goodman (wife of the Rev. Richard Goodman, vicar of Ballymodan, Bandon) was buried; and concerning whom it is related, that the sexton, being anxious to make his own a ring which was on one of her fingers, entered the tomb at night, and in his efforts to possess himself of the coveted jewel, awoke her out of the state of epilepsy she was in." (Another version of the same story claims that it was Mrs. Goodman's butler who tried to steal the ring).

The account does not tell what happened to the unfortunate sexton - or butler- who, albeit unwittingly, saved Mrs. Goodman's life, but the good lady herself returned to the arms of her shocked husband. She later gave birth to a son, John, who, apparently, grew up to be a bit of a vagabond spending much time in the taverns around Bandon cadging drink by telling the tale in graphic detail how he was the only person in the world who was born after his mother was buried in her grave. He died in Cork, aged eighty, no worse apparently, for his ordeal.

In the reign of Henry the Eight, Rosscarbery was part of the territory of McCarthy-Reigh. Towards the close of Elizabeth's reign. and after the disastrous defeat of O'Neill and O'Donnell at Kinsale, Archbishop Usher says:

"Florence McCarthy, notwithstanding the infinite favours and bounties which he had received from Her Majesty - being wholly

Spainiolized - had possessed the minds of those in Carbery and Desmond with a strange opinion of his worthiness; and having combined with Tyrone and other rebels when they were of late in Munster, did show himself in open action against Her Majesty. Whereupon the commissioners, Sir William St. Ledger and Sir H. Power, sent Captain Flower and one hundred horse, to make prosecution against the rebels of those parts."

On its way to Ross, he goes on to tell how the English army *"not only laid waste the country, but they contrived to lay hold of thirty-seven notorious rebels whom they executed. The whole country from Kinsale to Ross was so utterly wasted that there was neither horn or corn, or even a house left there to shelter a rebel; and from Ross to Bantry the country was similarly wasted."*

Rosscarbery, for centuries a haven for saints, warriors and rebels, was fittingly the scene where the final act in the bloody drama of the great Cromwellian Wars was enacted. On the 22nd of June, 1652, the town was surrendered to the English and an uneasy peace was concluded between General Ludlow on the side of Parliament, and Lord Muskerry on behalf of the Kilkenny Confederation.

In the vicinity of Rosscarbery stands Castlefreke, once the residence of George Patrick Evans-Freke. In the reign of Elizabeth, this branch of the Evanses possessed such wealth and influence in England that they were able to return eight members to sit in the English Parliament.

It is related that one of the Evans family on a visit from Rosscarbery to England, got into a heated discussion with some of his peers as to the antiquity of their various families. One claimed descent from a knight who had came over from France with the Norman invaders. Another claimed back to King Arthur and the Knights of the Round Table. However, the Rosscarbery gentleman proudly traced his ancestry back to a King who was, he declared, *"on the throne of Wales before King Arthur's grandmother had cut her first tooth."*

"Ah, indeed, sir," scoffed one of the group sarcastically, *"methinks you have spent too much of your time with the fairies in Ireland. No doubt you will tell us soon that your ancestors were with Noah in the ark."*

Castlefreke, Rosscarbery Bay.

Mr Evans drew himself up to his full height and bowed mockingly to his questioner.

"No Evans was ever reduced to such lowly circumstances," he declared haughtily, *"and I beg to acquaint you, sir, that, upon that memorable occasion, my people were on board their own yacht; and when sailing past the ark, Noah doffed his hat to them and said how delighted he was to find that his old friends the Evanses were safe and well."*

Like so many of the English who settled in Ireland, down the years, Mr Evans of Castlefreke had, undoubtedly, become *"wan of our own,"* and acquired the gift of the gab in the process. On the other hand, of course, it is firmly rooted in Kerry folklore that Noah's Ark ran aground on the Skelligs. Maybe, indeed, Noah did encounter the Evanses of Rosscarbery.....

Castlefreke, standing imposingly over the wide expanse of Rosscarbery Bay, was used as an army base during the Second World War. Regrettably its roof was removed in the 1950's for the value of its lead and timber and only the main walls stand proudly intact today.

Though, undoubtedly, Rosscarbery will always remember its pious son, St. Fachtna, with deepest affection, he was not the only Ross man who left his footprints in the sands of time. William (Philosopher) Thompson, a son of Rosscarbery is well known throughout the world as the Founding Father of the Co-Operative Movement, later called Communism (See Glandore). Tom Barry, one of the early IRA's most prominent Generals was born here in 1898, and General Michael Collins who, with others, negotiated and signed the 1921 Anglo-Irish Treaty which ended the long war with England and set up the Irish Free State was born near the town in 1890. (Nearby Clonakilty would also claim him as a son of theirs).

In 1921, frustrated and enraged at his inability to track down and kill Michael Collins, Lieutenant Percival of the British army, in command of a troop of Black and Tans, burnt down the farmhouse where Collins was born. What is left of the old homestead is now a National Monument dedicated to his memory. A year later, General Collins was ambushed and killed at Bael na mBlath by his own countymen. Twenty years on in 1942, the same Lieutenant Percival, then a General, ignominiously presided over the surrender of Singapore to an inferior force of Japanese. Lying off the coast of nearby Java, helpless to intervene, a strong British Eastern Fleet retreated to the safety of Ceylon. Coincidentally, this fleet was commanded by

Admiral Somerville, born and reared in Castletownshend. Rebel West Cork had spread its tentacles far....

Besides being a seat of learning, prominent for centuries all over Europe, Rosscarbery has always been a thriving seat of industry, holding fairs and trading farm produce. Today, the traditional fair lives on, being held each year in August. However, like so many other towns and villages in West Cork, Rosscarbery, during the summer months, depends on the tourist and the traveller, being close to many large and sandy beaches washed and warmed be the Gulf Stream currents. But the towering spire of St. Fachna's Cathedral and the memories which it evokes from an illustrious past will always be the crowning glory of Rosscarbery.

Castle Townsend

8

CASTLETOWNSHEND, GLANDORE, LEAP AND UNION HALL

Letter to the Editor of the Dublin Penny Journal. (Cork. August 21st, 1834).

"Sir: It has often astonished me, that while places far inferior to Castle Townsend are the resort of persons desiring sea-bathing, a spot so well calculated as this has been so long passed by. However, it is now, as it deserves, rising every day in importance, having been formerly composed of but a few fishing huts. It is now a neat pretty village - a new custom house as been built, and trade is beginning to flourish; slowly, indeed, at first, but I have no doubt that it will at length be frequented as a most desirable watering place. The foregoing is a sketch of the parish church, which has been lately built, and is situated in the splendid desmesne of Captain Townsend; it is taken from the opposite side of the bay, which runs up between two hills covered to the water's edge with trees. The harbour is capable of containing large vessels, notwithstanding which it is dangerous on account of rocks, which are under the water. I remain, Sir, your obedient servant, F.H.T."

Today, Castletownshend is a picturesque village with one narrow road falling steeply down to Townsend Castle and its small quayside. Check your brakes before you drive down it; there are two trees growing right in the middle of this narrow thoroughfare. They stand proudly erect as though they were sentries guarding the approaches to the ancient home of the Townsend family who built the first castle in this area in 1650. The little village itself grew up around the castle about the year 1745 and took the name Castletownshend.

Here too lived the Somervilles, a family long associated with the village and whose sons served honourably, over generations, in the highest ranks of the Royal Navy. One of them, a retired admiral in his eighties was murdered here in 1934 for allegedly recruiting local men for service in the Royal Navy.

In a totally different context, two highly talented members of the family, Edith Somerville and her cousin Violet Martin, the latter taking the pen-name Ross after her first home, Ross House in Co. Galway, collaborated in writing over 30 highly successful books. Amongst them, the hilarious series **"The Irish RM"** was serialised by the BBC and RTE. Originally called **"The Irish RM Complete"**, the stories are, today, recognised as classics in the field of Anglo-Irish literature. These talented ladies lived most of their lives in Castletownshend and even in death Somerville and Ross were not to be parted. They are buried in the neighbouring church of St. Barrahane.

Glandore is said to derive its name from the Gaelic Cuan Dor, meaning The Harbour of Oak, which tree was in former times so abundant all over Ireland and especially in the immediate neighbourhood of Glandore. Others claim that Cuan Dor means the Golden Harbour and the beauty of this tranquil village and its handsome harbour, coupled with the fact that it is reputed to have the mildest climate in West Cork, leads one to lean towards the latter suggestion.

According to Bennett, the great rebellion of 1641 made its first appearance in Cork in the village of Glandore where he states, *"several of the English were gagged to death, and where, in fiendish sport, the rebels forced a Presbyterian clergyman to eat a piece of his own flesh."*

Without doubt, there were many cruelties inflicted on innocent people by both sides and, depending on which history you read, once again you must make up your own mind on what or what not to believe. (Bennett was writing his history in the late 1800's and, strangely, the famine of the 1840's, through which he lived and witnessed, isn't even mentioned, though events such as the alleged rebellion atrocities in Glandore, two hundred years earlier, are chronicled in detail).

Not many people outside of West Cork know that when Karl Marx, the so-called founder of Communism was only twelve years old, a thriving Communist commune already existed in picturesque Glandore. This commune was set up by the wealthy, eccentric landowner Thompson of Rosscarbery around the year 1830.

Thompson was the son of a Cork merchant. He spend much of his early life in France and Belgium where he became exposed to the doctrines of the French revolution, and fell very much under the spell of the writings and theories of Voltaire.

Thompson owned a considerable amount of land around Glandore and, having a large fortune at his disposal, he decided to go ahead with his pet project which was, as he put it, *"the establishment of a community on the principles of mutual co-operation, united possessions and equality of exertions and means of enjoyment."*

Under the system he wished to establish, a number of people were to settle on his land which was to be divided into equal lots of one acre per person. Each individual was to bring in capital of from £20 to £100, depending on what he could afford, and each was to pursue the work for which he had been trained. All would work together for the good of the community, and each person's skills and output would be available free to the other members of the community.

The system appeared to work well under the general direction of Thompson. Unfortunately, he died in 1832. In his will he left the bulk of his

61

fortune to the community but the will was contested in law by his sister and declared invalid, as it was maintained that the property was willed for immoral purposes.

Whatever the good people of today's Glandore might think, the Glandore citizens of 1832 were not ready to accept what was one of the first principles of Thompson's theories - there would be no necessity for marriage ceremonies as there should be a community of wives as well as property. The Thompson project was quietly abandoned.

Fishery was once the basic industry of Glandore and the village had one of the largest fishing fleets along the coast. Today it depends more on tourism as its sheltered harbour makes it ideal for surfing and swimming. It was the first harbour to host an annual regatta as far back as 1830. This event is now an annual feature in Glandore's tourism calendar.

"At the upper end of Glandore Harbour," wrote Daniel Donovan in 1876, *"is a deep and dangerous glen called The Leap, on both sides of which is the high road from Ross to the other parts of West Carbery. The road crosses this glen which is here as steep as a flight of stairs so that few horses but those that are well used to it would attempt it with courage."*

One which indeed did leap across it was the horse of the legendary O'Donovan, a local chieftain, who when being pursued by English soldiers, made the daring leap across the daunting ravine and escaped into the wilds of West Carbery. No law agent dared enter this area which gave rise to the saying **"Beyond the Leap, beyond the Law."**

Today, Leap is a quiet village, a haven and resting place for tourists and travellers enjoying the beauty of West Cork. Its annual Festival of the Carberies provides two weeks of gaiety, dancing and song.

Union Hall, always a noted fishing village and now a delightful tourist centre as well as being the home port of the region's deep-sea fleet, is reached by crossing the metal bridge off the Glandore-Leap road. After the Act of Union of 1801 which joined Ireland as an integral part of Great Britain, the word Union was incorporated into many names, either of streets or towns to commemorate the importance of the Act. The Hall referred to was a large residence which dominated the village and of which nothing now remains.

The more ancient name for the village was Brean Traigh which translates roughly into Foul Strand. This name goes back to the more robust days of Irish history when the bodies of soldiers slain in battle were placed on the strand to be taken by the ebbing tide to a peaceful resting place in the depths of the ocean. The alternative name which appears in some old Irish documents is Traigh a 'Bhroin, the Strand of Sorrow, or as sometimes more beautifully translated, the Strand of Lamentations.

Whatever about the macabre connotations of the translations into English, the names Brean Traigh or more especially Traigh a'Bhroin fit more easily on the Irish tongue. Surely the time has now come when the residents of beautiful Traigh a'Bhroin should discard the meaningless English appellation, Union Hall, and let their ancient village take its rightful Irish place beside Cobh, Dun Laoghaire, Portlaoise and others which have long cast off the degrading mantle of imperialism.

9

CLONAKILTY

lonakilty, it is said, derives from Cloughneekeelty (the stone of Kilty). This stone, a replica of which now stands in Asna Square, is reputed to have come from the castle of a local Norman family of that name. Others suggest that the name comes from Cluan Keeltha (the harbour of the woods). Whichever derivation you choose, to the loyal citizens of this ancient town, the mere mention of the name, Joan Barry, brought with it waves of fear and revulsion and undying hate. Joan, a beautiful widow-lady from Muckross, and mother of David McPhillip Barry, a captain in the Irish army who fled Ireland to fight for France with the Wild Geese, twice led bands of women, as many as 400 strong, into the thriving town of Clonakilty and ransacked every house that was in it.

A writer of the time described the first invasion in 1642:

"There was no opposing these Amazons. With one weapon in their fist and another between their teeth, they could bewilder as well as pommel their antagonists. Quickly they overspread proud Clonakilty. Like a swarm of locusts they pitched upon everything. The curiosity and pillaging proclivities of Joan Barry's "Red Shanks" left nothing escape them. These unwomanly women stuffed everything into their bottomless pockets and when they walked off they left many a full heart behind them, and an empty shelf."

Even the militant feminist movement of the 90's would be wary of the proud Joan Barry, the angry Amazon of ancient Clonakilty.

Despite the fact that in 1292, Clonakilty received charter from Edward I to hold a market every Monday, it is reasonably certain that the town didn't really come into its own until it was occupied by some of those early settlers who came to the town of Bandon-Bridge towards the close of Elizabeth's reign, The names of many of its first inhabitants are common to both settlements. That they were English and that they professed the same religious and political opinions as their fellow-colonists at Bandon-Bridge, may be looked upon as equally certain.

In 1613 a charter of incorporation was granted to Richard Boyle, the Earl of Cork by which the inhabitants were incorporated as the "sovereign, free-burgessess and commonalty of the borough of Clonakilty." They also had the right to send two members to Parliament, but when the great rebellion of 1641 broke out, the town still had no walls to protect it and it was at the mercy of every passing marauder.

"Before 1641," wrote the historian Smith, *"the town flourished greatly, but being then burned down, it has since but slowly recovered."*

Gibson in his **"History of Cork"** tells us that at the outbreak of the Civil War in England in 1641, the English settlers in Clonakilty fled en mass to Bandon, which was a walled town. Lord Forbes, a Scottish nobleman, marched to Clonakilty, where he left two companies of Scottish troops and some Bandon militia to hold the town. He then pressed on to Rath-Barry. The Irish rose in his absence, and cut off the Scotch regiments but the Bandon men made good their retreat to an old fort near Ross. There they maintained their ground till reinforced by Lord Forbes. When they counter-attacked, the Irish were forced to retreat and made for Inchydoney in Clonakilty harbour, but the incoming tide cut them off and a large number of them were drowned. When Lord Forbes returned to the town, he found some of the English settlers imprisoned in the market- house, who firmly believed that they were to be burned alive in celebration of the victory of the Irish over the Scots.

In a tract entitled "**Good news from Ireland**", dated July 1642, one Ensign Jones reported as follows to Master Alexander Pollington in Lumber Street, London:

"From Bandon we marched to Clonakilty and found in the town not above twenty men, women and children, which our troops killed all, and ranged about, and found some hundred more hid in gardens and killed them all; then might you have seen every sex discovered, and some lying on their backs, old, young, none spared. At some sights I could have pitied...but I durst not cherish such a charity..."

With people about like the blood-thirsty Englishman, Ensign Jones, Lord Forbes, and the Irish lady, Joan Barry and her Amazon army, Clonakilty needed all the help it could get. However, politicians being politicians, whether in the 1990's or the 1690's, the help given to the loyal citizens of Clonakilty was, as usual, too little and too late.

In 1699, determined to show how well they looked after the morals of the people of Clonakilty, whatever about their physical well-being, the burgesses passed the following resolution:

"That Hanora Keliher is reputed to be a common whore, by having two bastards by two several persons, and we humbly decide as such that she be prosecuted..."

And to further prove that they also cared about the good health of the citizens, they went on to give a direction:

"that the dunghills that are now in the street, to the great nuisance of all the neighbourhood, be removed within three weeks: and that for the future, no dunghill lay in the street from the making of same under the pain and penalty of one shilling."

The provision and upkeep of the roads in Clonakilty always presented a problem to the politicians of the day. With no European Union funds to turn to for help, the loyal burgesses of Clonakilty found their own imaginative solution to the ongoing problem.

"We find and present," they said, *"that the road leading from Clonakilty to Timoleague - between the lands of Cahirgale, Gullames and Dorrery - ought to be repaired; and that three men out of each ploughland, living within the corporation, repair the same,"*

(That would, indeed, be a highly cost-efficient method of reducing our present dole queues).

And the burgesses were not going to be put off with any old back-chat from trade union officials or do-gooders about the unalienable rights of the individual.

"Should they or any of them refuse to come, they must pay one shilling each to be levied by the corporation constable. Mr. Herbert Baldwin and Captain Richard Hungerford to oversee the work, that it is properly done."

And as a final two-fingered salute to any trade union officials who might reside in the town, the instruction was *"that the said men should appear at work with their own spades and shovels."*

Charles Smith, writing in his *"History of Cork"* in 1815 had this to say of Clonakilty:

"Cloghnakilty is a town situated near the sea which affords it more pleasure then profit; the mouth of the harbour being choked with sand prevents vessels of burthen from coming up to the town. It is built in the form of a cross and there is a decent new church situated on rising ground. The country in the neighbourhood of Clonakilty is fertile and productive and there is a remarkable fair for all kinds of poultry on the 29th of September which supplies Cork, Kinsale, and neighbouring gentlemen and the shipping in both harbours with great quantities of

turkeys, geese, etc., and here also is a noted market for linen yarn which they bring in from West Carbery in considerable quantities."

Such prosperity, however, did not help the poor of Clonakilty when the dead hand of famine and plague spread out across the land in the dreaded late 1840's. It was then that the present hospital and Mount Carmel Home were built but Clonakilty witnessed many terrible scenes during the Famine period that earned the town the unenviable title, "Clonakilty God help us."

Writing in the late 1840's, it is recorded in Cork Constitution that *"on the 8th July, 1847 a hungry and demoralised mob of 300 people from the neighbourhood parishes descended on the soup rooms in Clonakilty Market House demanding food. Rations of rice, meal and 900 quarts of soup which were selectively being distributed were taken over."*

"Driven to a state of near frenzy at the arrest of 67 people by Lt. Redmond of the 54th Regiment from Clonakilty Barracks on the instructions of Thomas Allin, JP and their incarceration in the local Bridewell, an attempt was made to break open the jail. Having failed at this they returned to the Market House, hauled down the Town Clock and smashed it to pieces."

In his **"Sketches of Carbery"** in 1876, just thirty years later, Daniel Donovan summed up the new situation facing Clonakilty:

"The population according to the census of 1871 of Clonakilty is now down from a previous 12,000 to about 3,600. The cotton and linen manufacturers of the town formerly were more extensive, the latter affording employment to 400 looms and 1,000 persons, and the former to 40 looms. The weekly sales sometimes attained to the large sum of £1,000 . These manufactures, it is much to be regretted, have fallen to decay....."

The Great Famine had left its dread mark for ever on the town of Clonakilty. Today, the population of Clonakilty has fallen even further to

3000 people but this proud town wears its tragic past well. Walk through its streets where once weavers lived, and pass the Linen Hall where they sold their yarn. Mills, brewery buildings and quashed warehouses are around every corner recalling Clonakilty's once busy industrial and exporting past. Like the rest of West Cork, the people now rely mainly on a strong farming community and a burgeoning tourist trade for its main industry.

In this respect, some of the most interesting visitors ever received in the town flew in, as it were "out of the blue" on April 7th, 1943. They were, in fact, the crew of an American flying fortress which force-landed at the marsh between the mainland and Inchydoney. The crew of ten, a passenger and a pet monkey were accompanied to O'Donovan's Hotel by the local Defence Forces. They remained there for three days, the hotel and town taking on a carnival atmosphere as the visitors were royally feted in wartime Clonakilty. Eventually, a make-shift runway was laid and the plane took off for England. The monkey, "Tojo", was left behind and when he died he was buried in the garden of the hotel. The Warplane Research Group of Ireland erected a plaque on the hotel to commemorate the landing. It was unveiled on Sunday, July 17th, 1988 by Mr. Eddie Collins who was first to greet the crew in 1943.

Clonakilty's latest tourist attraction, an imaginative and unique Model Village will in the future be one of the most exciting tourist attractions in Ireland. Ireland's first theme Model Village will depict, in miniature, life and industry in West Cork as they were 50 years ago. The theme will be enhanced by the miniature working replica of the long closed West Cork Railway which served as the economic and social lifeline of the area.

Many of the industrial buildings which will be reconstructed in the Village had their own system of power generation during the era e.g. millwheels, etc. An All-Weather Interpretative Centre, located in the Park, will display mounted exhibits of the railway and the industries which once linked up the six West Cork towns of Bandon, Bantry, Clonakilty,

Dunmanway, Kinsale and Skibbereen, all of which will be reconstructed in miniature on a scale of 1.24 in the park

The Centre will be fitted with a state-of-the-art guidance control panel for the park's model railway which will contrast fully with the decor and exhibits in the interpretative area and 1940's style tea room. With Phase One, depicting Clonakilty and its past, successfully opened in 1994, this project promises to bring new life to Clonakilty's tourist trade.

In its short four hundred years of turbulent history Clonakilty has been pillaged and raped and burnt on numerous occasions by friends and foe alike and each time it lifted itself up to prosperity from the ashes of its past. Today, its inhabitants can look back to the achievements of their ancestors, the English, the Spaniards and the Irish. And even the name of Joan Barry can be recalled with pride.

A View of Kinsale
from the Old Fort
1750 –

10

Kinsale

"The town of Kinsale is a large stinking filthy hole, that hath nothing good in it besides honest Parson Tomms. I was glad to leave so vile a place, tho' indeed I was somewhat sorry to part with Parson Tomms, and the two only other fit gentlemen for Christian conversation beside himself in the whole town - viz., Mr. Stawell, and Parson Mead."

Thus wrote the Rev. Richard Allyn in his Journal dated October 23rd, 1691. So if there are any descendants of Parson Tomms, Parson Mead and Mr. M. Stawell still living in the town of Kinsale, stand up and take a bow. After all, Rev. Allyn, the chaplain of HMS Centurian, was a sea-faring gentleman who would surely know a good port of call when he saw one. He obviously wasn't very impressed by Kinsale and what it had to offer.

The name derives from the Irish, Ceann Taile, the head of the sea, alluding probably to the promontory called Old Head. Others suggest that the name comes from Cune Taile or Cune Saille which translates into "a smooth sea or basin". In some old Irish manuscripts the settlement is called Fan-na-Tuabred - the fall of the springs. Once again, the choice is yours.

Writing in his history of Cork, Smith says: *"This town is built under a hill, called Compass Hill, and extends about an English mile from the barrack at the north-east end (which is a handsome building for a regiment of men, pleasantly situated,) to the Worlds End, a place called on the south-west. A good number of houses are built on the side of this hill, and several also rise near its top, which from the bay and the opposite shore, make it look much better than it really is. This hill being of circular form, the place in a great measure takes its figure from it. The principal street, for want of room, is in many places narrow and incommodious. Over this are other street, but the communication is by steep slippery lanes, which, to strangers, are far from being agreeable. "*

Oh well, we must presume then that the Rev. Richard Allyn was, indeed, a stranger. Smith was writing in the year 1815, 124 years later, and he doesn't seem to have been very impressed by the town either. He quotes a verse written by Pope which he claims accurately describes Kinsale:

"And on the broken pavement here and there,.

Doth many a stinking sprat and herring lie;

A brandy and tobacco shop is near,

And hens and dogs and hogs are feeding by,

And here a sailor's jacket hangs to dry;

At every door are sunburnt matrons seen

Mending old nets, to catch the scaly fry,

Now singing shrill, and scolding oft between,

Scolds answer foul-mouthed scolds'

Bad neighbourhood I ween.. "

Smith was, however, impressed by the harbour about which he wrote as follows:

"The harbour is very commodious, being rendered deep and navagable by the river Bandon, which empties itself here, and with the advantage of its strong fort, makes it much frequented in war time. There are here a yard and dock for the building and repairing His

Majesty's vessels; also a crane and a gun wharf for the landing and shipping heavy artillery. Kinsale is the only port in Ireland where His Majesty's ships of war can be refitted."

Like the Rev. Allyn, Spanish fleets and armies would appear to have no reason to look back on their visits to Kinsale with any degree of relish or satisfaction. In 1380, in the reign of Richard 11, a Spanish fleet arrived off Kinsale and was decimated. An English historian, Thomas Walshingham, tells the tale:

"Spanish galleys did much mischief upon the coast of England; but about the latter end of June, 1380, a fleet of Englishmen from the West Counties forced them to retire and take harbour in a haven in Ireland called Kinsale, where, being assailed by the Englishmen and Irishmen, they were vanquished, so that to the number of 400 were slain and their chief captains taken. Five of their ships were taken and twenty-one English vessels were recovered, and but four of their captains escaped."

Two hundred and twenty years later, September 23rd, 1601, having apparently learnt no lessons, an army of 3,500 Spanish soldiers under Don Juan de Aquila landed again in Kinsale. An English army, commanded by Lord Mountjoy, immediately surrounded the town and penned in the Spaniards. Two months later, having achieved nothing, de Aquila sent urgent messengers north to the Lords O'Neill and O'Donnell demanding

"In the name of your church and your country, immediately march southwards and relieve Kinsale."

That plea from the gentleman who had come to relieve Ireland of the English yoke !

Ever eager to cross swords with their Saxon foes, the Northern Chiefs assembled their forces and undertook the long march south till they finally reached the village of Innishannon. There they were joined by seven hundred

Spanish troops who had arrived in Castlehaven, as well as the forces of many of the Munster Chiefs.

It is a measure of the hatred that O'Neill bore the English invaders of his country that it is recorded that when he was passing a castle on the line of march to Kinsale, he asked who lived there. When told that it was an Englishman named Barrett, who, however, was a good Catholic, and whose forefathers had been living in Ireland for the previous four hundred years, O'Neill declared, with an oath,

"No matter! I hate the churl as if he came over yesterday"

After some delay in Innishannon, the Irish forces moved down the left bank of the river Bandon and took up a position about a mile to the rear of the English camp, effectively cutting off all supplies and support from Cork. Thus, Mountjoy who was besieging Don Juan de Aquila in Kinsale, found himself besieged by the combined armies of O'Neill and O'Donnell.

The battle plan drawn up by the Irish and Spanish leaders was simple but, hopefully, an effective one. At dawn on the morning of Christmas Day, 1601, a day on which the English would least expect a Catholic army to attack, the Spaniards were to sally forth from Kinsale and assault the English front. At the same time the Irish would attack the English rear. But everything went sadly wrong.

It happened that the night of Christmas Eve turned out to be one of wild storm, heavy and constant rain, thunder and lightning, snow and gale-force winds. And an informer, the curse of Irish history down the long years, had warned Mountjoy of the exact timing of the impending assault. Accordingly, when day broke, the Irish army which expected to fall upon a sleeping foe, found that the English, already under arms and drawn up in battle array, were ready and waiting for them.

Out-numbered and out-gunned, the forces of O'Neill and O'Donnell were as powerless as a flock of sheep. The slaughter was great. Many Munster chieftains who had joined forces with O'Neill were killed. The bodies of over twelve hundred Irish soldiers were counted on the field of battle and many more perished in retreat. And the Spanish army, 3,500 strong, in Kinsale, disheartened and dismayed at the ferocity of the weather, took no part in the battle.

O'Donnell fled to Spain to seek further help and O'Neill returned to Ulster. He remained there until 1607 when he and his kinsman were forced through continuous English harassment to flee Ireland for ever. Don Juan de Aquila surrendered with his army on the 2nd January, 1602. The terms of the shameful capitulation read as follows: *"That the Spanish should evacuate Kinsale, Castlehaven and Bearhaven, that they should have liberty to carry into Spain all their arms, ammunition and treasure, and that they should be provided with shipping and victuals to transport them if they paid for the same."*

In the six short months the Spaniards were in Kinsale they had managed, through their inaction and cowardice, to reduce the Irish people to total serfdom, After what became known as The Flight of the Earls in 1607 when the O'Neill's and the O'Donnell's fled to Spain, the northern counties were opened to the plantation which, even to this day, is still a blight on the Irish nation.

No story of Kinsale would be complete without reference to the Lady in White who is said to haunt the ruins of Charles Fort, so called in honour of King Charles the Second. William Robinson, architect of the Royal Hospital, Kilmainham, Dublin is credited with designing the fort which continued to be garrisoned until 1921.

Historian Smith tells us that *"construction of the fort was started in 1670 and was finished at the expense of £73,000. On the works to the sea are one hundred pieces of brass cannon mounted, carrying from twenty-four to forty-two pound ball. The embrasures are all bomb-proof. This fort is so situated that all ships coming into harbour must sail within a pistol shot of the royal battery. It stands one mile east of Kinsale, and hath a regiment of foot always quartered in it."*

A governor of the fort at one time was a Colonel Warrender, a strict disciplinarian who handed down the death sentence for even minor breaches of discipline. He had an only daughter, whom he adored, with the rather unusual name of Wilful and she had just married Sir Trevor Ashurst. They were walking along the battlements on the evening of their wedding when Wilful espied some wild flowers growing on the rocks below *"Oh, Trevor,"* she said coyly, *"how lovely they are and how I wish I could get some of them."* Sir Trevor may or may not have been a chivalrous man but before he had time to reply, a sentry, on duty beside the spot, volunteered: *"If you wish, Sir, I shall climb down and get the flowers for your lady, but you will have to act as sentry while I am away. If the Governor should come around..."*

His offer was accepted and he hurried away in search of a rope while Sir Trevor donned the long cape and shouldered the musket. Wilful found the evening air going chilly and returned to their room. The rocks below the battlement were sharp and slippery and the soldier found the job wasn't nearly as easy as he had thought. Time went by and Sir Trevor, his brain dulled, no doubt, by the liberal drafts of wine he had consumed at the wedding feast, dropped off to sleep. Unfortunately, just then the Governor did his rounds.

He came to the sitting sentry and challenged him. There was no reply. The Governor barked again. But there was only the murmur of the restless waves on the rocks below. Governor Warrender drew his pistol and, without hesitation, shot the sleeping sentry through the heart. Brusquely, he ordered some soldiers to carry the body inside and thus the tragedy was discovered. At that moment, Wilful returned to see what was delaying her husband. When she saw his dead body, she screamed and, rushing away from the small group who tried to restrain her, she threw herself over the battlements on to the rocks below.

Her father, the Governor, overcome with grief, retired to his quarters and shot himself. So a bunch of wild flowers growing on the rocks below Charles Ford had brought about a triple family tragedy in a matter of minutes. Since then, down the years, many people claim to have seen the Lady in White wandering distraught amongst the ruins of Charles Fort, searching, searching, ever searching. Like the Spaniards, she is now part of the tragic history of Kinsale.

When references are made to the Crimean War, 1854 -'56, most accounts recall the Charge of the Light Brigade and the charitable exploits of the famous Lady of the Lamp, Florence Nightingale.

Nothing much is heard of the extraordinary achievements of a group of Irish Mercy Nuns who became known as the Kinsale Nuns. They volunteered in response to an appeal sent to all the Mercy Convents in Ireland wherever there were nuns experienced in nursing. It fell to Mother Francis Bridgeman in Kinsale to make up and lead a party of 15 nursing sisters. The sisters went on to earn the highest praise for their nursing skill. The last word came from Dr. John Hall, Inspector-General of Hospitals:

"The superiority of an order system is beautifully illustrated in the Sisters of Mercy. One mind appears to move them all. Their intelligence, delicacy and conscientiousness invest them with a halo of extreme confidence. The medical officers can safely assign the most critical cases to their hands....."

Kinsale nuns were ever ready to stand up and be counted. It was the Superior of the Carmelite Convent in Kinsale who during the Great Famine of 1847 complained bitterly to Mr. T. N. Redington, the Under-Secretary, that the starving people of the town were being given so-called "soup" made with only ten ounces of meal and rice to a quart of water, and that the four-ounce slice of bread which went with it was very small because the bread

79

was made with one-third Indian meal which weighed heavy. *"You are deliberately killing off the people,"* she declared, *"and on your head be it..."*

But all that was long ago. Nowadays, *"Kinsale for Fabulous Fishing"* has long been a slogan for the sea anglers of the world. A very wide variety of other sea-based sports are also available. Oysterhaven, just 6 miles from Kinsale, is Ireland's major windsurfing centre. Kinsale also offers a scubadiving school with breath-taking dives off the Old Head of Kinsale. The Yacht Club hosts many international events inshore and offshore during the sailing season. Quaint and ancient buildings still rise from narrow winding streets while the harbour itself is one of Irelands most scenic harbours and is port-of-call to a large number of foreign visiting craft.

And apart from its water amenities, Kinsale, today, proudly boasts that it is now the gourmet capital of Ireland and has a proliferation of small owner-run eating establishments. In fact, it is claimed that it is possible to spend up to two weeks in the town and dine in a different top restaurant every evening.

In 1995, Kinsale was awarded the coveted title of being Europe's top holiday and environmental resort, and in the final shake-down shrugged off the challenge of the U.K's Peak District National Park and other tourist parks in Austria and Germany.

EU Commissioner Christos Papoutsis described Kinsale as *"a striking example of how to turn an urban architectural heritage into a tourist attraction."*

In 1996 Kinsale was named as the first winner of the 32-County Tidy Town Competition.

"Everybody is pulling together from the school children to the council members," Committee Chairman Danny Cummins, reported proudly.

I do believe that even that prejudiced old sea dog, the Rev. Richard Allyn might gladly have changed his mind about Kinsale if his spirit still wanders that lovely port's narrow bustling streets....

11

Skibbereen

aking a rather colourful, if charitable comparison, Daniel Donovan in his **"Sketches of Carbery"**, published in 1876, said: *"Skibbereen, before 1631, was a puny village - like Rome in its infancy."* Now there's something that should make the present population of Skibbereen sit up and worry. Where, in fact, have they gone wrong? How and when did Rome so obviously outstrip them?

The significance of the year 1631 in Skibbereen's history derives from the fact that it was then that Algerian pirates descended on nearby Baltimore and sacked that ancient town. Those of the more wealthy inhabitants lucky enough to escape the sword or captivity and slavery, fled Baltimore for ever and settled in the neighbourhood of Skibbereen, and from this period, says Donovan, *"we must date the enrolling of Skibbereen upon the list of notable and rising towns in the south of the county of Cork."*

The name of Skibbereen, or Skubbareen, unlike Rome is of doubtful origins - historian Dr. Joyce suggested that it meant *"a place of skiffs."* These skiffs used to ply across the rivers Ilan and Caol before the erection of the bridges at the Steam Mill and Abbey. What is fact, however, is that Skibbereen and its adjacent countryside was formerly a portion of the demesne surrounding Gortnaclohy Castle and belonged to McCarthy Reigh of Kilbritten.

In the time of Cromwell, the McCarthy estates were forfeit after the great rebellion of 1641, and Skibbereen and the lands of Gortnaclough, Smorane and Coronea were granted to William Prigg and Samuel Hall. The patentees, like so many others who got grants in those days, were very anxious to obliterate the old names and so they renamed the town, New Stapleton. It is by that name that it is referred to in the patent which mentions *"Skibbereen, to be for ever called New Stapleton."*

Under its new name, the town is mentioned in the patent obtained by Prigg and Hall in 1681 for holding two fairs (one on the feast of St. Peter, the other on the feast of St. Andrew), and two markets, one on Wednesday and one on Saturday. There was also a patent for holding fairs granted to Richard Townsend dated March 1, 1778. The earliest date in which the town of Skibbereen can be found in Irish annals is that of 1544 when Florence Magther was presented to the rectory and vicarage by Henry VIII, *"the late incumbent being an Irishman."*

Dr. Dive Downs, who was Protestant bishop of Cork during the end of the 17th century, once decided to make a tour of his vast diocese on horseback, the roads being too narrow and impassable for carriages. He visited Skibbereen in 1699 and stayed the night at the house of Lady Catherine Barclay at Bridgetown.

"The church of Skibbereen," he wrote, *"was formerly the markethouse and was consecrated about the year 1686 by Dr. Wetenhill, Bishop of Cork. It stands in the parish of Abbeystrowry and the Earl of Orrory has the entire impropriation."*

That, in effect, meant that the unfortunate local vicar had no formal income and was therefore obliged to change rather hefty and unusual fees for his own upkeep. The good bishop goes on in rather shocked fashion to outline some of those fees: *"When the man of a family, or a widow, dies worth more than five pounds, the sum of thirteen shillings and four pence is demanded as a mortuary, and if he dies worth less than five*

*pounds, then his second best suit of clothes must be handed over, or six
shillings in lieu thereof...*"

AbbeyStrewery Church, Skibbereen.

As he doesn't specify what happened to the unfortunate man's best
suit, one can only assume that the corpse was buried in it. The good
Bishop concludes: *"The church in which divine service was performed
was burnt down in the reign of James the Second but was put in good
repair in 1695 at a cost of twenty pounds."*

With prices like that, it is little wonder that the vicar settled for second-
hand clothes.

In his **"Sketches of Carbery"** Donovan says that the population of
Skibbereen had *"decreased considerably within the last thirty years - it
was previously nearly 5,000 and is now only 3,700, a decrease to be
attributed to the Great Famine and consequent emigration."*

Gibson, too, in his History of Cork, states that *"no part of Ireland suffered more or lost more of its population during the famine years than the town and district of Skibbereen."*

On the other hand, in the early 1800's an extensive trade in the manufacture of woollen and linen cloth as well as basic agricultural produce formed the mainstay of the people's livelihood. In the records of the Rev. H. Townsend (1815), the town is quoted as having a bolting mills, porter and beer breweries and an extensive distillery of whiskey. Why then should famine so cruelly and extensively devastate the town and environs of Skibbereen?

For the most part, the Irish peasant lived off a tiny piece of land for which he paid such a high rent that almost all, and sometimes all, the cereal crops he grew on it had to be sold to pay the rent. He and his family subsided on a plot of potatoes. When the potato crop failed in the late 1840's, disaster struck the Irish peasant and his family. They just had no money to buy the available foodstuffs. If they didn't pay the rents, mostly to absentee landlords, they were evicted from their holding.

It is, of course, one of the great paradoxes and tragedies of the Famine Period that even more misery was brought about by bureaucratic pigheadedness on the part of British civil servants, one particularly, Charles Trevelyan. Permanent Head of the Treasury. It was he who insisted that, because of the rules of political economy, even though every sort of food except the potato was readily available in Ireland, such food should not be distributed free to the starving people.

"Such a practice would undermine market prices and disturb market forces," he argued, *"and must be actively discouraged. The people must work for what they receive."*

And so numerous public works at very low wages were started all over the country - roads which didn't need to be straightened were straightened, walls, where no walls were required, were built but still the overcrowded workhouses were filled to capacity.

Worse than the low wages was the fact that owing to bureaucratic delays, wages quite often were not paid at all. At Skibbereen men were working on the roads, weak and exhausted for want of food, without being paid for a fortnight. When the body of a labourer who had been employed on the public works was found on the road just outside Skibbereen, the coroner's jury found that he had met his death *"for want of sufficient sustenance for many days previous to his decease, and that this want of sustenance was occasioned by his not having been paid his wages on the public works for eight days previous to the time of his death."*

It is, another strange paradox of that fateful period that Skibbereen was always noted as a centre of food production second to none in the county of Cork. Says historian George Bennett of Bandon: *"Skibbereen is known as a seat of the provision trade - large quantities of butter, corn, pigs and cattle being annually disposed of in its weekly markets and fairs. It is very advantageously situated for a trade of this kind in the centre of a wide and improving district, and only two miles distant from where the river is navagable at Old Court for vessels of two hundred tons burthen. Facilities are afforded by this waterway of exporting its produce..."*

Confirmation of this can be gleaned from the fact that at about the time the people of Skibbereen were dying of starvation, a vessel arrived in Cobh carrying 5000 barrels of Indian corn-meal from Boston for the starving Irish. It was met by Father Matthew in the Mayor's barge and both officers and men were taken on a pleasure-cruise around the harbour.

Afterwards, a dinner was given for the officers in Cork and the sumptuous menu offered turbot, salmon, spiced beef, rump of beef, hares, tongues, pigeon pies, lamb, chicken, duckling, turkeys, lobster salads, veal, haunch of mutton, sponge cakes, jellies, creams, ices, blancmanges, pies, tarts, cheese cakes, tartlets, grapes, apples, plums, cherries, strawberries, all washed down with champagne, claret and port. It is not recorded what the surprised officers bringing food to the starving Irish thought of such lavish hospitality.

No doubt much of this exotic food was produced in the dying town of starving Skibbereen. Meanwhile, Skibbereen's famine victims were heeled by the cartload into a communal grave in the Abbey Cemetery west of the town where to-day the visitor can still view the Famine Plot. And still the exports of foodstuffs rolled out through the port of Cork. It is also on record that money collected abroad by charitable bodies and sent to Skibbereen to buy food for the starving inhabitants was in fact used to transport them to England and Wales where they were then shipped on to Canada and America.

History, as we must keep reminding our readers, is sometimes nothing more than the prejudiced view-point of the writer. Bennett's history, written at his home in Bandon and published in the year 1869, makes no reference to any famine in Skibbereen or, for that matter, anywhere else in Ireland.

Little wonder, then, that when Jermiah O'Donovan Rossa founded the Phoenix Society in 1856 to demand an Irish national identity for Ireland, the Society was immediately suppressed by the British authorities. The Skibbereen members of the Society imprisoned in Mountjoy Gaol outnumbered those from any other town in Ireland. Equally, it was a Skibbereen man, Gearoid O'Sullivan who raised the national flag over the GPO in Dublin in 1916.

The degradation and sufferings of the famine years of 1845-1849 scored an indelible mark on the minds and memories of Skibbereen people. This has remained with them for generations, not only in West Cork but in far-flung countries throughout the whole world where coffin ships deposited them far from their homeland.

Much controversy was stirred up over the years in Skibbereen, and, indeed, all over Munster, by the two weekly newspapers which the town managed, uniquely, to support since the 1800's. The "Skibbereen Eagle", founded in 1857 and the second oldest provincial newspaper in Ireland, will always be remembered for its editorial threat to the Czar of Russia that the Eagle "was keeping a close eye on him". Protestant-owned and extremely anti-Irish, it was soon opposed by the "Southern Star" founded in 1889 by a young nationalist.

After years of attack and counter-attack, in September, 1920 the Eagle's premises were raided and most of the machinery destroyed. In January, 1929, what remained of the Eagles premises and machinery was sold to the Southern Star for £1,400 cash. The Southern Star, noted for the number of times it was suppressed for its nationalist views, continues to flourish throughout Munster today.

Lough Hyne.

About four miles from the town, the beautiful Lough Hyen, the only inland salt-water lake in Northern Europe, is a constant source of joy and wonder to visitors both Irish and foreign. About 1 km long and 3/4 km wide, the tidal rise and fall within the Lough is 1 metre. Outflow lasts 8½ hours and inflow lasts 4 hours. Low tide is 3½ hours later than that of the sea.

Surrounded by towering wooded hills and mountain, Lough Hyen presents itself as a tranquil shimmering mirror to be admired and enjoyed with pleasure and a deep sense of awe that nature could create such glorious grandeur from a wilderness so vast. On an island in the centre of the lake are the remains of a castle built by, of course, an O'Driscoll.

In recent years, in conjunction with a still strong farming industry, but especially since the establishment of the West Cork Development Association, life and hope have returned to a Skibbereen denuded by famine and emigration over the long, sad years. Skibbereen is once again as it was described by Daniel Donovan in the 1870's *"a busy centre of trade occupied by an intelligent, enterprising and industrious population."*

Tourism too has become an important factor in the lives of the people of the town which is so centrally located in the scenic beauty of West Cork. It is of little wonder that the town's Welcome Home Festival, run for ten days every year in late July, attracts people from all over the world. Unfortunately, since those dread famine days the people of Skibbereen are from all over the world... .

12

Bantry and the Beara Peninsula

n officer of King James, writing in 1689 said: *"Bantry is a miserable poore place, not worthy of the name of a town, having not above 7 or 8 little houses, the rest being very mean cottages."*

Oh, well...!

Bantry derives its name from the Gaelic, Ban-tra (white strand), the white, shingly foreshore in front of the town. Other opinions hold that it derives from Beant Mac Fariola, a descendent of the O'Donovans and O'Mahonys, the two septs who formerly possessed all this country.

Fable has it that the first person ever to reach Ireland from the Continent was a lady who landed at Donemark, (Dun na mBarc - the fort of the ships), a few miles to the west of Bantry. She was Caesar, daughter of Bith, son of Noah and she led a group of 3 women and 24 men. Though the fact is not recorded, no doubt the good lady came to pay a courtesy visit on her grand-daddy's old friends, the Evanses of Rosscarbery.

More than any other European country, France and her armies have played a major role in the history of Bantry over the long years of war and rebellion. Lord Orrory suggested in 1665 that the towns of Bantry and Berehaven should be carefully guarded. Not only did their harbours afford a secure retreat for the descent of an enemy fleet, he claimed, but the surrounding countryside was inhabited by a large hostile population ready and anxious to cast off the yoke of England.

"I know no other place in Ireland," he complained in a letter to the Lord Lieutenant, *"so fit to begin a rebellion as is this place- both for the multitude of ill-people in it, the fastnesses of the country, and the good unguarded harbours in it, from whence, out of France, they may be there in forty-eight hours."*

In another letter he said that West Carbery contains *"great crowds of ill-affected Irish."* And again, that in those parts of Carbery, Beare and Bantry, *"he was assured that there was a great number of the worst sort of people in Ireland - that they were ready for any villainy. I am certain,"* he observed astutely, *"that there is no such a pack of rouges in all Ireland as those in the west of this county of Cork,"*

Whether or not the present inhabitants of Bantry and its environs would agree with the opinions held of their noble ancestors by the good Lord Orrory, I know not. He was right, however, about the dangers of invasion from France.

In 1689, the Count de Chateau Reined cast anchor in Bantry Bay and landed a supply of money and military stores for the use of King James the Second. The English Admiral Herbert, based in Kinsale, had been ordered to see that no assistance should reach Ireland from France. When he heard that the French were in the bay, he immediately put to sea and though greatly outnumbered - the French Fleet comprised twenty-eight ships of war and five fireships - Herbert sailed in to attack. After a brief encounter during which some broadsides were exchanged and no damage was done to either side, Herbert judiciously stood out to sea and the Frenchman drew in closer to shore.

That night, under cover of darkness, the French fleet slipped out of Bantry Bay. Herbert's look-outs saw them going but the wily admiral, his task successfully concluded as far as he was concerned, wisely allowed them to go unmolested. Later, safely back at their home ports, both sides claimed a great victory. The House of Commons passed a vote of thanks to its admiral for what, to make the most of it, was a mere skirmish, if skirmish it could be called. King James, for his part, was so overjoyed that he had bonfires lit, and a Te Deum chanted in honour of the great victory gained over the English fleet by the French.

Need we remind the reader again that history is quite often no more than fable and tale passed down through the centuries, filtered or polluted by local interpretation? Take it or leave it as you see fit.

On the 22nd of December, 1796, a more formidable French fleet arrived in Bantry Bay. Owing to a thick fog, the French ships were able to slip by the English fleet on constant patrol off Kinsale, but many were scattered. On board, the French had fifteen thousand soldiers under the command of General Hoche, together with *"one thousand, one hundred and sixty stands of arms, twenty pieces of field artillery, nine large siege guns, mortars, howitzers, sixty-one thousand two hundred kegs of powder, seven millions of ball cartridges, seven hundred thousand flints and a motley supply of small arms."*

Rebel West Cork and Bantry in particular, waited with bated breath. The long-awaited liberation was at hand. The French, at last, were in the Bay.

Wolfe Tone, the founder of the United Irishmen, was on board the Indomitable, a formidable fighting ship of eighty guns. His diary entry for December 22nd, 1796 said:

"This morning at eight o'clock we have neared Bantry Bay considerably, but the fleet is terribly scattered." And four days later, December 26: *"Last night, at half past six o'clock, with a heavy gale of wind still from the east, we were surprised by the admiral's frigate running under our quarter, and hailing the Indomitable with orders to cut our cable and put to sea instantly. The frigate then pursued her course, leaving us all in the utmost astonishment. All our hopes are now*

reduced to get back to the safety of Brest. Well, let me think no more about it. It is lost and let it go ... "

Gibson, in his **History of Cork**, wrote of the event:

"Wolfe Tone did as much as any man could do to conquer Ireland by French bayonets, in order that it might be converted to French and republican opinions, or to anything but what it was. He bore an undying hatred to the English rule. He would, he said, 'rather that France, Spain, the Autocrat of Russia, or the Devil himself, had the country, than England',"

History does not record the reasons why this mighty French army failed to land in Bantry having successfully made the hazardous journey from Brittany. Whatever the reason, the fleet sailed away into the turbulent darkness on the night of December 26th, 1796, and returned to France, having remained off Bantry for just six days. Wolfe Tone's greatest attempt to rid his country for ever of the hated English invader had come to naught.

What history does record, however, is the sad fate of a small dog belonging to Mr. James Sweeney of Bantry. On that fateful morning in 1796, Mr. Sweeney was walking his dog on the hills above the stormy seas. Looking out across the bay he saw the billowing sails of more than 50 French men-of-war looming out of the early morning mist. Hastily he gathered up the dog, a spaniel puppy named Pompey, and with him safely tucked under his cape, he hurried to Bantry to report the arrival of the French fleet to Richard White, the Commander of the British forces in Bantry. White immediately ordered Sweeney to ride with all haste to Cork to warn the authorities there of the imminent invasion by the French army.

Mr. Sweeney, who was born and reared in Bandon, was chosen because he, better than most, knew all the short-cuts through the wilds and forests of Carbery and he accomplished the hazardous journey in a day and a night, having used up three horses almost to the point of death. What Mr. Sweeney didn't know, unfortunately, was that, in his hurry, he had forgotten to lock up Pompey, before he set out on his journey, and the little animal, in his loyal love, had followed him all the way from Bantry to Cork.

Having passed on his information to the authorities of the invasion by the French, Mr. Sweeney returned to the stable where he had left his horse. A Bandon historian of the time writes:

"To his utter amazement and dismay, he found his little pet lying on the saddlecloth in the stable, prostrate and gasping for breath. Upon seeing him, poor Pompey made an attempt to get up and greet his old master as usual, but the effort was too much for him; he fell back and after a few feeble struggles he was dead. Mr. Sweeney carefully wrapped poor Pompey in the cloth on which he lay; and on his way back to Bantry he had his family burial-place in the churchyard of Ballymodan opened, and with his own hands he laid the remains of his faithful little companion amongst the dust and ashes of his kindred."

The same historian, writing of the fishing industry in Bantry had this to say:

"In 1749 Mr. Richard Meade, an enterprising fishmerchant in the town, proved to the satisfaction of the Dublin Society that he caught and cured on his own account, in that year, no less than three hundred and eighty thousand fish of various kinds; and Mr. James Young, another trader, saved, the previous year, two hundred and thirty-one barrels of sprats, and four hundred and eighty-two thousand herrings. When the fishing was good, Bantry prospered; but when the fish ceased to frequent the bay and the coasts adjoining, for whatever reason, the town gradually kept sinking from bad to worse. Pilchards, herring, haak and sprats were at one time taken in great abundance; but for the last fifty years the take of fish of any kind did not pay the expenses. Now, a valuable strand, thickly strewn with coral, and a tourist traffic in the summer months, are the chief support of Bantry."

It was a sad coincidence that at this time the Famine had begun to stalk the land and even Bantry, which previously had a seemingly inexhaustive harvest of food in its seas should now feel the brunt of misery and hunger.

A report from Bantry workhouse, dated October 1847 which was already housing "2,327 persons and 600 children, naked except for filthy rags, half-starved and without the common decencies of life" had this to say:

"Our town at six o'clock this morning was a scene of unparalleled misery and destitution. At that early hour two hookers arrived at our quay laden with 240 human spectres from Berehaven who had quitted their homes of wretchedness to find shelter in the workhouse. I saw them crawl from where they landed...I saw them cling with tenacity to the outer gates; he who was so fortunate as to grapple with the iron railings kept his place till one of the Guardians arrived who secured admission for the famished applicants. Here even our misery does not terminate - the resources of the Union are exhausted and the establishment is in debt to a fearful amount....Let Ministers no longer deceive themselves by vainly imagining that the local resources of any Union in Ireland would be sufficient to maintain its poor. If they regard us as fellow subjects and wish to snatch us from the jaws of death, let them interfere without loss of time...."

A Protestant clergyman, the Rev. F. F. Trench described what were called "trap coffins" which he saw in Bantry:

" ...the bottom is supported by hinges at one side and a hook-and-eye at the other. In these coffins the poor are carried to the grave, rather to a large pit, which I saw at a little distance from the road, and the bodies are dropped into it. But I was told in this district the majority were taken to the grave without any coffins and buried in their rags; in some instances even the rags are taken from the corpse to cover some still living body..."

The sad fact of life was that the curraghs of the West Cork fishermen were totally unsuited to deep-sea fishing and their miserable in-shore catch was usually sold to buy potatoes. When the potatoes failed, those same fishermen had to pawn or sell their curraghs to buy meal to feed their families.

Today, at the entrance to the town stands Bantry House one of the most famous of Irish stately homes, having been the seat of the Earls of Bantry since Richard White was elevated to the peerage in 1797 in reward for his services during the French invasion.

Advanced to the dignity of Viscount White in 1800, he became Earl Bantry and Viscount Berehaven in 1816. The title became extinct in 1892 when William Hare White, 4th Earl, died without male heir and the estates passed to the female succession.

Bantry House is now open to the public and is full of treasures, many of them from the palace of Versailles, collected mainly by Richard White, 2nd Earl of Bantry, on his extensive travels in Europe in the 19th century. They include four panels of Royal Aubusson tapestry which were made for Marie Antoinette on her marriage to the Dauphin. There is also a Gobelin tapestry and wainscoting of 17th century Spanish leather, brightly painted and embossed, as well as chests from the Indies, and urns from the Orient. The Second Earl is also reputed to be responsible for laying out the formal gardens.

The Armada Exhibition Centre is sited at the East Stable. Open to tourists since 1991 it includes a new visitors' shop and it tells the graphic story of the 1796 Armada's disastrous attempt to overthrow the English forces in Ireland. Left behind in that attempt was the veteran frigate "La Survellante" - too storm battered to make the voyage back to Brest, she was scuttled off Whiddy Island on January 2nd, 1797 and has lain there undisturbed for over 200 years.

Rediscovered in 1982, Surveillante was declared an Irish national monument in 1985 and the work began on its recovery, conservation and exhibition. The centrepiece of the exhibition is a 1 to 6 scale model of the frigate in cross-section, showing her construction and the various activities that were happening on board, vividly illustrating life in the French Navy 200 years ago. The centre also contains a fine collection of Maritime artefacts.

The Beauties of Glengarriff

Unfortunately, there is no mention of the tragic part played by the little Bantry dog, Pompey, in that fateful invasion. The irony of the fact will not be lost on the visitor that the Exhibition, which commemorates Wolfe Tone's attempt to rid Ireland for ever of the English forces he hated so much, is now housed proudly in the stately residence, albeit the former stables, of the descendants of his arch enemy, Richard White, Earl of Bantry.

Farther along the coast of Bantry Bay is the sheltered harbour of Glengarriff and Garnish Island. This little island is known the world over as an island of rare beauty. What was once a bare rocky island of holly and birch scrub has been transformed into a paradise which is alight with rhododendrons and azaleas in Spring and a riot of cultivars, climbing shrubs and herbaceous perennials which dazzle the eye from June onwards. Centrepiece is the Italian Garden, formal and colonnaded with terraces and pools. This is surrounded by a wild garden and a long glade called the Happy Valley.

Nowadays, Bantry is very much a town dependent on its markets, its fishing fleet and the tourist industry to make it the thriving town it has become. No doubt too, many of the tourists visiting Bantry are French. As well as the French Armada Centre, they will, probably, visit the ill-fated oil storage terminal in Whiddy Island which once received the world's largest oil tankers until the tragic disaster in 1979 when the French tanker, "Betelgeuse", exploded with the loss of 50 lives, The jetty installations were destroyed putting paid to Whiddy Island as an oil storage depot. Since then, Bantry Bay has become one of the most productive fish farming locations in Western Europe employing over 100 people.

There is a monument to the dead French sailors in the Abbey Cemetery. While our French tourists will always be made feel very welcome, one hopes, without appearing ungracious, that they spend more time in our midst and contribute more to the well-being of the town's inhabitants then did their ancestors of yore. Once again, the wheel of history has turned full circle.

Castletownbere, also called Berehaven, the principal town of the Beara Peninsula, was developed after the copper mines were founded in Allihies in 1812. It then became a British naval base and retained a British naval presence as one of the Treaty Ports until the arrangement was terminated in 1938. It is now one of the main bases of the Irish fishing fleet.

Near the town once stood the castle of Donal Cam O'Sullivan-Bere who dominated the Beara Peninsula and in the latter years of the 15th century commanded all insurgent forces in Munster, numbering over 2,000 men.

O'Sullivan-Bere had readily rallied his clansmen and neighbours to join with O'Neill and O'Donnell in the ill-fated campaign against English rule which terminated with the battle of Kinsale in 1601. After the defeat at Kinsale the Spanish commander Del Aquila treacherously surrendered not only Kinsale town to the English forces of Carew but also the castles in Castlehaven, Baltimore and Dunboy which had been taken over by Spanish soldiers to hold them safe for their Irish owners. O'Sullivan-Bere found himself in the unusual position of having to storm his own castle, Dunboy, to recover it from the Spanish forces who were supposed to be his allies.

Some months later, however, the English recaptured Dunboy and O'Sullivan, eventually surrounded on all sides by hostile forces, both English and Irish, decided to march north to his cousin, O'Rourke of Breffny in Leitrim and seek refuge there. On December 31st, 1602, he and 1,000 of his clan, comprising 400 fighting soldiers, camp servants, women and children set out on the long march north. They left behind them the old and those too ill to travel. Three days later the English General Wilmot arrived from Kenmare with an army of 5,000 men to destroy O'Sullivan-Bere once and for all. In his angry frustration when he found that his quarry had flown he ordered his men to slaughter all those unfortunates whom O'Sullivan had been forced to leave behind.

O'Sullivan finally arrived at O'Rourke's castle on January 14th having survived savage attacks by English armies as well as Irish chieftains whose land he had marched through. Of the 1,000 of his clan who had set out so hopefully from the Beara Peninsula only 90 survived the long hostile march. The rest had been killed or died of hunger and exposure.

After resting for some weeks O'Sullivan marched on to join up once again with the forces of O'Neill whom he had fought beside at the battle of Kinsale. He found to his profound dismay that O'Neill had already surrendered to the English. Rather than accept the humiliation of surrender, O'Sullivan-Bere fled to Spain where he died, a broken and disillusioned man, in 1616.

The ruins of Dunboy Castle - not to be confused with the Dunboy Castle built in the 19th century by the Puxley family, who owned the coppermines in Allihies - can still be seen today, a proud monument to the most illustrious of all the Chiefs of Munster, Donal Cam O'Sullivan-Bere.

13

Baltimore and Carbery's Hundred Isles.

ack in the 1930's our history teacher, a saintly Christian gentleman but an avowed Anglophobe, was ever ready to pour hatred, scorn and ridicule on anything and everything English. On reflection, he was hardly the best person to shape and form the young minds of a learning generation. Looking at the famous, or infamous, Sack of Baltimore of June 20th, 1631, he constantly quoted soulfully and sadly from the poem by Thomas Davis:

"From out their beds, and to their doors rush maid and sire and Dame,

And meet upon the threshold stone, the gleaming sabres fall,

And o'er each black and bearded face the white or crimson shawl,

The yell of 'Allah!' breaks above the prayer and shriek and roar,

O blessed God, the Algerine is Lord of Baltimore."

We wept with him there in the classroom as he outlined in gory detail the terrible fate suffered by our kith and kin, butchered at the hands of the barbarous Algerine in Baltimore. Had our history teacher known then, as I know now, that Davis had written his poem from the depths of his sentimental imagination rather than any recognition of historical fact, and that the 100 or so of Baltimore's residents kidnapped into terrible slavery were, in fact, English settlers, then we would, no doubt, have been joyfully cheering on the side of our glorious allies, the infidel Algerine. History, unfortunately, is never a thing of black and white; there are always shades of grey.

Baltimore was, in olden days, a celebrated sanctuary of the Druids and at that time known as Dunashad - the Fortress of the Jewels. Later it became known as Baltimore from the Irish words, Baile an Ti More - the town of the great house. As far back as the beginning of the 16th century it was described *"as a town of considerable importance and a great resort and haven for fishermen from the ports of France and Spain."*

Unfortunately, the savagery of Ireland's history was never kind to Baltimore, and especially the name of Fineen O'Driscoll, sometimes known as Florence, will live forever in the annals of that fair town.

"The O'Driscolls were brave sailors," wrote Gibson in his **History of Cork,** *"and they owned every acre of Carbery before the English invasion."* He added, with tongue in cheek, perhaps; *"They also did some successful trade in the pirating line."*

The merchants of Waterford, more than any others, had reason to hate the O'Driscolls of Baltimore. In 1573, Fineen O'Driscoll and his son, Gilly Dubh, the Black Boy, spied four vessels beating about in a storm that raged over the south coast of Ireland. They immediately took to their own boat and went aboard the La Sancta Maria de Soci, which was heavily laden with rich Portuguese wine, and offered to pilot the ship into harbour in exchange for three pipes of the precious liquid. The offer was gratefully accepted, as was the subsequent invitation to the captain and crew to dine at O'Driscolls castle, Dun-na-long, on Sherkin Island. There they were treacherously clapped in irons and the ship was plundered of its cargo of 100 pipes of wine.

The wine had been consigned to Waterford merchants who, on hearing of the fate of their expensive cargo, fitted out an expedition to revenge the dastardly deeds of the Pirate Driscoll. A force of 300 men under Captain Woodlock landed on Sherkin, ravaged the island, destroyed the village and a

Franciscan friary that had been established there, and also besieged the Castle of Dun-na-long which they took by storm. They burnt all the galleys and pinnacles belonging to O'Driscoll and went on to set fire to the town of Baltimore.

Fineen O'Driscoll was, by all accounts, a loveable rogue and recognising in him, perhaps, a kindred spirit, he was well liked by Queen Elizabeth. This came about when in the middle of her reign, an English fleet lay becalmed off Baltimore. Unlike his treatment of the Portuguese, O'Driscoll ordered out all his galleys and boats and towed the ships safely into harbour. Once again he invited the officers and crews to join him at dinner in his castle.

Writes a historian at the time:

"There was eating and drinking; there was dance and song. Wine and money were everywhere. In the wantonness of his mirth and hospitality, the host ordered the town well to be cleared out, and for forty-eight hours kept it filled with wine. And as an inducement to the avaricious as well as the thirsty to visit the flowing bowl, he had fistfuls of gold and silver thrown into it; hence the name- Tobber-an-Argid (the money well)."

So pleased were the officers with such bountiful and hospitable treatment, that, when they returned to England, they told Her Majesty about the way they were received in Baltimore. And so grateful was Elizabeth that she wrote a letter to O'Driscoll, thanking him for his hospitality and inviting him to come to London to see her.

Unfortunately for Fineen O'Driscoll, in the insurrection of 1601 he allowed the Spaniards to occupy his castle and when Kinsale surrendered, the castle and lands of the O'Driscolls and all their possessions both on the mainland and on the islands were declared forfeit to the crown. Fineen and his family fled to Spain.

By the year 1631, the town, now occupied by English settlers, had regained most of its former wealth and glory but the merchants of Waterford still remembered the wrongs done to them by the men of Baltimore. On the terrible night of June 20th, 1631 a Waterford man named Hackett piloted two Algerian galleys into the Harbour and before the sleeping inhabitants realised what was happening, the town was sacked and over 100 of its people, men, women and children, were captured and taken off into slavery.

The following account of the assault was supplied by Dr. Caulfield to the editor of the Munster Journal:

"Their commander, Matthew Rice or Reis, advanced to the town with one hundred and forty of his 'Turks', leaving sixty musketeers in ambush along the road, and taking with him John Hackett of Waterford as a guide. He carried the place by assault, and surprised the English inhabitants breaking into forty houses, of which they plundered thirty - seven. They would have continued their work of devastation, but a man called William Harris was wakened by the noise, looked out of his house and perceived that, the place was overrun by 'Turks', he fired several shots and arousing the neighbours, drums were beaten in the upper part of the town and Reis and his men fell back on their forces in reserve and thence to the vessels but they did not weigh anchor until four o'clock in the afternoon when they then took their prisoners into cruel slavery in North Africa...."

Wrote Thomas Davis:

"Oh, some must tug the galley's oar, and some must tend the steed,

This boy will bear a Sheik's chibouk, and he a Bey's jarreed

Oh! Some are for the arsenals of beauteous Dardenells;

And some are in the caravan to Mecca's sandy dells..."

Revenge, however, is always sweet if not completely satisfying. Two short years later, the treacherous Hackett of Waterford was captured and brought back in chains to Baltimore. There the remaining inhabitants hanged him by the neck on the cliff facing the sea and looking down on the short channel through which he had piloted the pirate Algerians. Baltimore had its revenge but it never recovered from the cruel blow that had so savagely struck on that dread night of June 20th, 1631. Most of the remaining inhabitants retreated back up the river Ilen and settled in Skibbereen. Writes historian Charles Smith:

"Baltimore never recovered itself since this accident; it is now a poor decayed fishing town with not one tolerable house in it; here are the ruins of the ancient castle of the O'Driscolls." And, as if to add salt to the wounds, he finishes: *"The late Right Hon. John Calvert, esq, Baron of Baltimore, who was proprietor of the province of Maryland and Avalon in America, took his title from Baltimore in the county of Longford, and not from this place, as has been mistaken..."*

Smith too is mistaken when he refers to the ruins of the ancient castle of O'Driscoll in Baltimore village. This castle was subsequently built by English settlers to repel any further Algerian incursions.

The infidel Algerine and Hackett of Dungarvan will never be forgotten as long as the proud town of Baltimore, for centuries reduced to poverty and ruin, looks out onto the sea.

Today, Baltimore is a picturesque coastal village and a tourist mecca with its pretty houses perched on the side of the steep cliffs that once looked out to sea in search of pirate or invader. And in the noisy quite of a Baltimore pub the tourist may still hear the soulful ballad telling the tragic fate of O'Driscoll's daughter in an Algerian harem:

"They came on shore and caused great slaughter

And carried off O'Driscoll's daughter.

Behold her anguish; also her fears

A poor captive carried into Algiers.

Whilst in the harem she stood alone.

And the sun above her brightly shone.

To her flattering tales the Pasha told

And showed her his pearls and gold.

But the virtuous maid, nobly born,

His love and his treasures she did scorn

By force she was by him caressed

But she plunged a dagger in his chest... "

This may well be so, but it is also darkly hinted that the Algerians had inside information regarding the defences of Baltimore supplied by O'Driscoll himself, then living with his family in exile in Spain and thirsting for revenge on the English invaders who had deprived him of his birthright. And despite the tragic ballad lamenting the fate of O'Driscoll's daughter in an Algerian harem, it is more likely that she was happily bedded down in the luxury of a Spanish castle. History as we keep insisting, sways with every breeze and panders to the listener's fondest dreams.

Needless to say, the ravages of the Great Famine spread from nearby Skibbereen to the village and environs of Baltimore. Subsequently, to keep the life and soul of the village together, a Fishery School to promote boat building and navigation was opened in the grounds of the present Beacon Park Hotel. A thriving fishing industry developed and pilchards, herring and mackerel were pressed for oil and a steady and lucrative export market was developed. Special fish trains - as many as 16 per day left Baltimore for Cork right up to the outbreak of the First World War. In 1920 the slump in the American fish market caused many of the operatives to emigrate. The School closed in 1951 but a year later a boat building yard was established by Bord Iascaigh Mhara which survived until the late seventies and kept the town alive. Today, there are four different boat building enterprises between Baltimore and upriver Oldcourt near Skibbereen.

The famed hundred isles of Carbery dot the surface of Roaring Water Bay, that beautiful expanse of water that stretches out before Baltimore but which is so frequently lashed to vicious turbulence when a south - east or southerly gale whips in from the wild Atlantic. Smith in his **"History of Cork"** gives the following strange account connected with these islands:

"In the latter end of March 830 A.D. there happened such terrible shocks of thunder and lighting in this area that above 1000 persons were destroyed by it. At the same time the sea broke through the banks in a most violent manner and overflowed a considerable tract of land...."

He then goes on to suggest that;

"It is not improbable that, taking into account the peculiar conformation of Sherkin and Cape Clear and the other islands that dot the bay, the great elevation of the land, the similar direction of the coast line, and the very narrow distances which separate the islands from each other and the mainland, that the whole lot may have originally projected into the sea as an unbroken promontory, in the same manner as the Mizen Head."

Though this vast tract of land could well have been converted into islands by the constant action of the seas, it is more likely as Smith suggests, *"that it was caused by that violent convulsion of nature"* - an earthquake - nearly 1,500 years before.

And there are fishermen in the pubs of Baltimore who, over a pint when the short Autumn evenings close darkly down around the village, will tell tales to the visiting tourist that on such a moon-lit night when the fishing fleet is out past Cape Clear towards Fastnet, the shadowy outline of the legendary lost city of Atlantis can sometimes be seen on the far distant hazy horizon.

Atlantis, they will assure the tourist, was the capital of West Cork and stood majestically on the promontory swept away in the disaster of 830 AD. And they will assure him further, as, hopefully he buys another pint, that a castle built by an O'Driscoll is the dominant feature of the Atlantis sky line.

Cape Clear, the largest of Carbery's Hundred Isles, has now a population of 200 people whereas it supported over 1000 before the Great Famine. It was here that Saint Kiernan was born in 352 AD, before Patrick ever came to Ireland. From here too came St. Fachtna, later the founder of Rosscarbery Abbey.

"The inhabitants of these islands," Dr. Smith writes, *"are generally a very simple and honest people, thieving being a crime very little known to them. If a person be found guilty of a crime, he is directly banished to the continent, which is the greatest punishment they can inflict on the criminal who endeavours all he can to remain on the island..."*

On the south west of the island stands the ruin of another O'Driscoll castle, Dun an Oir (The Castle of Gold). After the battle of Kinsale, O'Driscoll was forced to surrender the castle to the English crown, and stories and fable still abound about the gold and treasure buried under the ruins. So far none of it has been recovered. Like the famed city of Atlantis, it too is part of the folklore of today's Baltimore.

Baltimore is now a thriving tourist town with dingy-sailing in the harbour, deep-sea diving, deep-sea fishing and traditional pubs and restaurants with traditional food as well as traditional songs - not all of them accurate, as we have pointed out, as far as O'Driscoll and his daughter are concerned. But foreign tourists from as far afield as America, Spain, France and Italy, as well as England and, who knows, Algeria itself, are all now very welcome in this, the ancient fortress of the famed O'Driscolls.

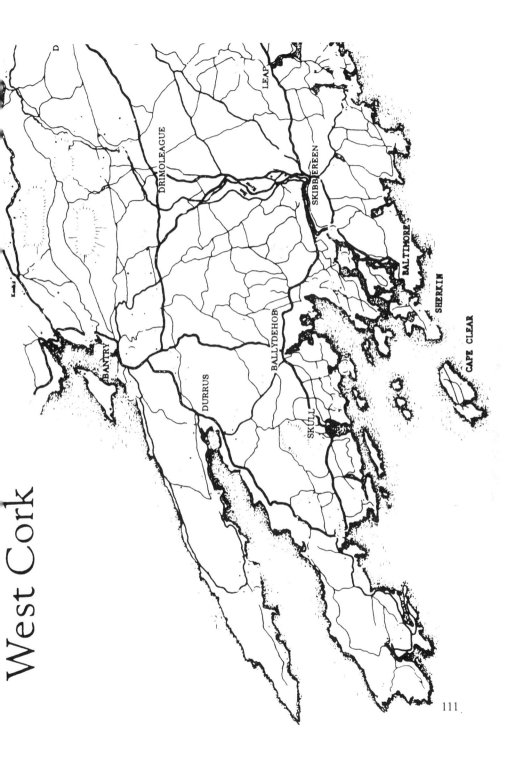

West Cork

Main St., Schull.

14

Mount Gabriel, Schull, Ballydehob, Crookhaven, Mizen Head and beyond....

cull, wrote Historian Charles Smith, *"is but a small, insignificant village, having few buildings besides the church and parsonage house. To the north of it stands a high conical hill, called Mount Gabriel; on the top of it is a remarkable lough which is but a few yards broad; it has been sounded from the north - east with one hundred fathoms of line; although the lead stopped, yet the hole was deeper, it being choked up with a long coarse grass. The water oozes out of the mountain to the north - east, and this cone is above 300 yards higher than the level of the sea; from it can be seen a noble prospect of a vast extent of rude uncultivated country from the Mizen Head to Ross..."*

The present residents of Schull would refute Smith's description of their beloved village. Today's tourist literature says that: *"Schull has become, in recent years, one of West Cork's most popular resorts. The village lies at the foot of Mount Gabriel providing a superb backdrop to a scenic harbour, one of the finest along the South West Coast. Summer sees the village come alive with tourists as is has expanded its holiday facilities and the area is excellently served with numerous accommodation outlets...."*

It was not, unfortunately, always such a happy village. In 1846 at the height of the famine, fever raged around Skull and Ballydehob, the latter another charming village lying to the east of towering Mount Gabriel. Ballydehob's greatest claim to fame is its towering 12-arch viaduct and the fact that it was the birthplace of the 1930's world wrestling champion, the great Danno Mahony.

How many died in this area during the famine years will never be known as the residents were so terrified that they could make no effort to help those who were dying (See Appendix). One report, however, commends the Ladies' Associations of Skull and Ballydehob who, *"with great courage and self - sacrifice were visiting even the worst cases and distributing food and clothes. "*

Ireland's oldest pick and shovel have recently gone on display at Fitzgerald Park in Cork in an exhibition entitled "Our Mining Heritage" and it is confirmed that they were recovered from archaeological excavations at Mount Gabriel and date back to between 1700 and 1600 BC. Also on display are stone hammers and examples of bronze and copper axes. Strangely, the pick and shovel were made from timber.

Metal mining apparently began in West Cork 4,000 years ago with the introduction of copper bronze metallurgy. In fact, West Cork's Bronze Age copper mines are amongst the best preserved examples in Europe. There were important mining districts in West Carbery and the far end of the Beara Peninsula. Several hundred mine sites are known from this period. From 1812 onwards an increased interest in these mining districts led to a very careful examination of the area by Cornish miners with copper the chief target. The largest and best preserved Bronze Age copper mine is on Mount Gabriel and some 32 primitive workings have been discovered on the mountain.

Mount Gabriel, 1339 ft. high, commands a panoramic view of the Mizen Peninsula and is easily identified from a distance by the two giant "golf balls" standing on its summit. These "golf balls" are part of a European - wide network of communication systems, monitoring air and sea traffic in the North Atlantic.

Not to be outdone in the technological field by its towering neighbour, Schull village boasts of a Planetarium, the only one in the Republic of Ireland. In addition to showing the night sky in its 8-metre dome it can also show it as seen from any part of the Northern Hemisphere at any time in its past history. Scull and Ballydehob, in the shadow of Mount Gabriel go back a long way.....

To the west of Schull stands the picturesque village of Crookhaven where lies the ruin of the radio station from which Marconi sent his first radio message to America. Further west still, Mizen Head towers a full 700 feet high, its lighthouse being the most southerly point of Ireland and where in the hazy Summer days the sharks may be seen basking in the warm sunny seas.

With Mount Gabriel towering to the sky and Mizen Head reaching out to the throbbing Atlantic, this is the south - west border of West Cork. America and Canada, home to many an Irish exile, lie far over the horizon....

Bibliography

The History of Cork - Gibson (1860)

History of Bandon - Bennett (1869)

Sketches of Carbery - Daniel Donovan (1879)

History of Cork - Charles Smith (1815)

History of Cork - Charles Smith with additional notes from the Croker and Caulfield Manuscripts (1893),

edited by Robert Day and W. A. Copinger

Dunmanway - a Local History - Pupils of the Vocational School,

Dunmanway. (1993)

The Whiskey Distillers of the United Kingdom (1887)

The Dublin Penny Journal (1834)

Realities of Irish Life - W.S. Trench (1868)

APPENDIX

1. Names of settlers planted in West Cork and decreed by Queen Elizabeth that they be *"English and Protestant and their heirs were to marry none but of English birth" :-*

Abbott,	Clark,	Evans,	Greenway,	Jifford,
Alcock,	Christmas,	Ellwell,	Gardiner,	Joyce,
Adderly,	Carey,	Elliot,	Glenfoild,	Kerall,
Atkins,	Crofte,	Elms,	Giles,	Kite,
Austen,	Cox,	Flemming,	Grenville,	Kent,
Bernard,	Cotterall,	Fondwell,	Greatrakes,	Kingston,
Baldwin,	Clear,	Franck,	Grimstead,	Light,
Brayly,	Cooper,	Farre,	Hewitt,	Little,
Bennett,	Chipstow,	Flewellan,	Harvie,	Linscombe,
Birde,	Cable,	Fenten,	Holbedyr,	Law,
Beamish,	Cleather,	French,	Hodder,	Langford,
Brooke,	Churchill,	Franklin,	Howard,	Lapp,
Blacknell,	Cecill,	Fuller,	Hussey,	Lissone,
Burwood,	Dolbers,	Fryher,	Hitchcock,	Lambe,
Berry,	Drake,	Frost,	Hill,	Lucas,
Booll,	Downs,	Grant,	Harris,	Lane,
Bramlet,	Dunkin,	Grimes,	Hales,	Lake
Blofield,	Daunte,	Gamon,	Hammett,	Monoarke,
Coomes,	Davis,	Griffith,	Hardinge,	Moaks,
Corkwell,	Deane,	Green,	Jones,	Mowberry,
Chambers,	Dun,	Goodchild,	Jackson,	Meldon,
Cadlopp,	Dashwood,	Grimster,	Jumper,	Martyn,

Margets,	Rashleigh,	Scott,	Thompson,	Whaley,
Newce,	Radley,	Savage,	Taylor,	Wight,
Newman,	Rake,	Skinner,	Thomas,	Williams,
Nelson,	Richmond,	Skence,	Tobye,	Wheeler,
Osmond,	Spenser,	Shephard,	Tucker,	White,
Porter,	Symons,	Smith,	Travers,	Woodroffe,
Perrott,	Synoger,	Spratt,	Tanner,	Ware,
Poole,	Stanley,	Seymour,	Valley,	Warren,
Pitt,	Skipwith,	Sweete,	Vick,	Willobe,
Peyton,	Snookes,	Sugar,	Vane,	Watkins,
Preston,	Saunderss,	Tickner,	Woolfe,	Wheatley,
Popham,	Skipwith,	Turner,	Wiseman,	Wade.

Algerian Pirates sack Baltimore.

he following is a list of the names of the persons kidnapped from Baltimore by the Algerian pirates in 1631 and carried off into cruel slavery. It was never established if any of them managed to return to Ireland, or what their fate in captivity was....

William Arnold - wife and three children	5
Micheal Amble - wife and son	2
John Amble	1
Stephen Brodbrook - wife and three children	4
Corrent Crofine - wife, daughter, and three men	6
Cooke-wife and maid	3
Edward Cherrye	1
Robert Chimon - wife and four children	6
Mrs. Corlew - wife of Timothy who was killed	1
Bob Evans - and boy	2
William Garter wife, maid and seven children	10
John Harris - wife, mother and three children	6
'Ould Hanniken - wife and daughter	3
Bessie Flood and son	2

William Mould and boy	2
Dermot Mergy - two children and maid	4
Richard Meade - wife and three children	5
Christopher Norway - wife and child	3
'Ould Osborne and maid	2
Alice Hearld	1
Stephen Pierse - wife, mother and three children	6
Thomas Payne - wife and two children	4
Bessie Peters - and daughter	2
Alexander Punnery - and wife	2
John Ryder - wife and two children	4
Robert Hunt - and wife	2
Abram Roberts - wife and four children	6
Richard Larg - wife, sister and four children	7
Sampson Rogers - and son	2
Morris Plower - and wife	2
William Symons - wife and two children	4
John Slyman - wife and two children	4
Richard Watts - wife and two children	4
Total	119

Of these, Ould Osborne and Alice Heard were deemed by the Algerian pirates to be passed their sell-by dates and were thrown overboard. Fortunately, they managed to swim to the shore and were saved.

Total Baltimore prisoners 117

Origins of the West Cork Brogue and Dialect.

ecently in Dunmanway, Co. Cork a man who the inhabitants of the town would describe as a "mountainy man" pointed at the nearby telephone box in the Square and said to me in disgust: *"I cud na get ere a shpake outa dat Ould yoke."*

I knew exactly what he meant, not because I too had earlier failed to get *"ere a shpake"* out of that particular telephone, but because that was the English we spoke in West Cork 70 years ago - like: *"dis wather is cauld, ax yer Mudder to hate it up agin."*

This was the English that despairing school-masters had tried to beat out of us over the years, and not always with any great degree of success. And today, this is the English that our purists and elocution teachers would dismiss as "stage-Irish". And, of course, they blame it on the inability of the native Gaelic speaker of yore to get his tongue around those weird English Th.'s and vowels. But I wonder if that was really so?

It is interesting to note that in the list of the natives of Baltimore who were kidnapped by Algerian pirates in 1631, two were named as "Ould Hannikin" and "Ould Osborne". Baltimore was an English plantation, so why "Ould" and not "Old"?

Writing in 1869, Historian Bennett records a conversation between the inhabitants of Bandon - *"all stoutly English and all stoutly Protestant"* -

when the first Irishman, Paddy Gaffney, was allowed to open a shop in Bandon-bridge:

"Yaw! Where bees ye goin, Sammy?" says one old fellow to another, who was trudging past his door on his way up to Paddy's.

"Be dad, Johnny, up to see de live Papist data's cum to live near the prate-market!"

"Laws, man, a live Papis?"

"A live Papis!" chimed in another neighbour, with wonder spreading in his eyes. *"Janey, Dick,"* calling out to a friend who had just put his head out of a window, *"sure ye niver he-ard sich news! Dere's a live Papish here !"*

"Is it de French is coming agin to Bantry Bay?" eagerly enquired an old woman.

"Naw, Betsy, it ain't, bit tis what's a great dale worse - dere's a live Papish cum to live in de straat."

"Be dis and be dat," she groaned mournfully, "de end of the world can't be far off so..."

So whatever our purists may argue, it seems that what is now referred to as our quaint West Cork dialect, or dismissed out of hand as stage-Irish, is, in fact, the English spoken by the Elizabethan settlers from Devon, Cornwall and Somerset who colonised West Cork and from whom the native Irish learnt the English language

And if Bord Telecom had been operating in Bandon-bridge in the 1700's, those good staunch Englishmen would have understood exactly what the Dunmanway mountainy man meant when he said he couldn't get ere a shpake outa dat ould yoke.

Famine in West Cork.

The following letter, written by the Rev. F.F.Trench, Perpetual Curate of Cloughjordan, Co. Tipperary to the Editor of the "Examiner" in March, 1847, will afford some idea of the horror and misery inflicted on the inhabitants of West Cork by the Famine.

Sir: My attention was first directed to the famine in Schull by Captain Caffin. It was painful to myself and others to think that within two or three days' journey from our homes thousands of our fellow-creatures should be dying of absolute starvation. It was therefore proposed that I should visit those locations with a view to administering such relief as appeared most judicious and practicable. I accordingly did so and have just returned.

The account which Captain Caffin gave of what he saw in Schull seemed too dreadful to be true, but there is one broad and astonishing fact which indisputably proves that it was far, very far, below the truth and that is that every family which Captain Caffin visited, and of which he writes, was a Protestant family. Dr.Traill, the Rector of the parish, stated this to me. Now it is well known that in every part of Ireland the Protestants are a wealthier class than the Roman Catholics. If here, then, the Protestants are in a state which Captain Caffin describes, what must be the condition of the Roman Catholics? Dr. Traill himself said to me, after returning to the hovels to which he accompanied me - "until today I did not know the real state of the people."

In travelling through the parishes of East and West Schull, containing the villages of Ballydehob and a population of about 16,000 people still living, I did not see a child playing in the streets or on the roads; no children are to be seen outside the doors but a few sick and dying children.

Captain Harston, the agent of the British Relief Association, informed me that on Sunday, March 7 , he had seen a woman with a basket on her back, and the crooked corpse of a child fastened outside it. Dr.McCormick, the dispensary physician, stated that on Tuesday, March 9, he had met a man, a father, tottering along the road, a rope was over his shoulder, and at the other end of the rope, streeling along the ground, were two dead children, whom he was with difficulty dragging to the grave.

Mr. O'Callaghan, of Kilmanus, informed me that he used meal bags for burying people; graves are frequently made in ditches, and corners of the fields, and in the gardens behind the cabins. I saw in one garden, not far from Ballydehob, close to the mail-coach road, two graves in a garden - one large, in which I was told were three bodies, the smaller one in which there were two bodies; and the house had been burned, in consequence of the whole family, nine in number, having died in it of fever.

I then proceeded to Cappagh, which is a coast-guard station, in the midst of a starving population, which had been collected around mines which are not now being used. It was proposed to establish the first eating-house in this place. On the evening before, I had heard of a boy living on the road to Cappagh, who had seen a dog tearing at the head and neck and ribs of a man. I wished to learn the truth of this from the boy himself. He told me that the fact was so, and that his little brother had on another occasion seen another dog tearing the head of a man. The younger boy remarked that he had seen the remains of the head the day before in an adjoining field. I asked him to lead me to the spot and I there found a part of the human head and under-jaw, gnawed, but marked with blood. I placed it underground.

In the afternoon of the same day I proceeded in company with Mr. Barry, the Roman Catholic priest. I asked him to point out to me the most distressed houses. He said, "In every direction, it is all the same."

In the first house I entered there was a man lying in fever, and wife and child sitting up. I found the door shut. A young man who lived near told me that he had not seen the door open except once or twice in the last fortnight. There was a can of water near the bed: four of the family had died. The sick people said they had eaten nothing that day; I immediately sent to a farmer's house at a little distance for some oatmeal, and gave some to them and took the remainder with me.

In the second house I entered (Patrick Driscoll's) there were eight in family; three sick; one man lay dead beside the fire. I asked did he die of fever? "No, sir, of starvation," was the reply.

Third house (Regan). Here I heard the groaning of a sick and (I was told) a dying man. The place was so dark I did not go in far. Eight in family; pictures of death. Two girls and a young child said they had eaten nothing all day. Mr. Barry told me the man had been a decent farmer.

Fourth house (Widow Driscoll). Here I saw a young man. He was groaning and it appeared to me in the agony of death. There were five in the family. They said they had eaten nothing since Saturday, i.e. for two days and a half. They were all sick; all were swelled; and the priest with me said, "None of them can live."

Fifth house (Matt Sullivan). We knocked here. None were able to open the door. Two very young children sitting by the fire, and two lying pale as death.

Sixth house (Widow Cunningham). She had buried her husband and her three children. She had been ill for eight weeks. Her last boy had taken fever the day before. She had no one to go for anything now. The last drink she got was a jug of water from a woman going along the road and knew not where the next would come from.

Seventh house (Phil Regan). He had died and the widow was dying. Their three children had died. She was awfully swelled.

Eighth house (Paddy Ryan). Eight, all sick. One had died. Child scarcely able to open the door.

Ninth house (Charles Regan). Of eleven only three remaining. We had met the woman of this house on the road and she accompanied us to most of the houses. When we arrived at her cabin, she said, "I have within a fine young man of nineteen years of age, and you could carry him in the palm of your hand." I entered and saw a bundle of skin and bone naked and partly wrapped up in a blanket, sitting by the fire. The mother said, "Sir, we have no sickness but hunger."

I had seen enough. These houses were not all in a row, but scattered in the fields and along the roadside. I did not pass by a single house. Turning around I said to Mr. Barry, the Roman Catholic curate, "Are the houses I see further down just as bad?" He said, "They are, sir; and all along the place; they are in fact worse below. I have come from a house there in which I saw two stretched..."

Before I conclude I wish to mention the very small cost of these eating-houses which we have endeavoured to establish here. I have before me the cost of five of the eating-houses, and I find that 9,409 substantial meals have been given at an average cost of less than a penny farthing each. The lives of the people in this district seem to be marvellously given into our hands, and who can tell what a blessed influence our charity may have upon their spiritual welfare. Yet while deprecating in the strongest possible manner the holding out of any carnal inducements to the reception of spiritual good, and while loathing from my innermost soul the iniquity of holding out to the miserable to do that which their poverty and not their will might consent - still I say who can tell the extent to which in this very district the Saviour's word may be fulfilled - "Let your light so shine before men that they may see your good works and glorify your Father which is in Heaven."

I remain, dear Sir, yours faithfully and obliged,

F.F.Trench, Perpetual Curate of Cloughjordan.

INDEX